Assessment:
The Cornerstone of Activity Programs

Ruth Perschbacher, ACC, RMT-BC

Assessment:
The Cornerstone of Activity Programs

Ruth Perschbacher, ACC, RMT-BC

Venture Publishing, Inc. • 1999 Cato Avenue • State College, PA • 16801

Library of Congress Cataloging in Publication Data
Author: Ruth Perschbacher, ACC, RMT-BC
     Assessment: The Cornerstone of Activity Programs

Production: Bonnie Godbey
Printing and Binding: BookCrafters
Manuscript Editing: Michele Barbin
Graphic Design: Naomi Q. Gallagher

Library of Congress Catalogue Card Number 93-85327
ISBN 0-910251-62-2

10 9 8 7 6 5 4 3 2 1

FOREWORD

Bristlecone pines are the oldest, continuously living things on earth. They grow in the Western United States at timberline, one of the most rugged terrains and climates. When a Bristlecone tree is first spotted, it appears to be dead, but as one draws closer, the life on the ends of the branches becomes obvious. Likewise, the elderly, particularly the frail elderly, are too often viewed from the perspective of being near death, yet as we draw closer, the lifetime of experiences and wisdom is evident. Therapeutic activity programs create an environment that cultivates the well-being in each individual. This book describes how activity professionals can create opportunities to assure that the elderly will continue to partake of the fruits of life.

Human beings merit full recognition of their selfhood throughout the life span. Holding sacred the individuality of each person in long-term care depends on the willingness of professionals in geriatrics to break loose from the traditional medical model and begin to focus on abilities, strengths, and wellness. Well-educated consumers are already beginning to demand services that go beyond basic physical care. Individualized activity programs offer opportunities and choices so that residents can pursue their lives with dignity and a sense of self-worth. To claim full actualization, activity therapy programs must be recognized as forceful players in the care of the elderly. Special attention and resources should be committed to these programs. Administrators, nurses, social workers and other caregivers need to expand their awareness of how activity programs and activity professionals affect the lives of residents. Activity programs engage the attention and energy of individuals and provide a healing force that cannot be underestimated. Exploration of this force has only begun; this book is a part of the exploration. The future of activity programming holds a great deal of hope for meeting the challenges of aging in a manner which exemplifies the sanctity of life at every point of the spectrum.

ACKNOWLEDGMENTS

The author wishes to thank a number of people who took part in this book's long journey. Margaret Hartman, Director of Special Services at GreenTree Ridge in Asheville, North Carolina, Letitia Jackson, Coordinator for Project Life at the University of Missouri, and Natalie Frost, Director of Activity Therapy at Hillhaven Rehabilitation and Convalescent Center in Asheville, North Carolina, reviewed the first edition and provided guidance for aspects of the second edition. Each of these women has played a significant role in influencing and challenging my thinking about the value of therapeutic activity programs. Janet Wells, Director of Publications for the National Citizens Coalition for Nursing Home Reform, reviewed the first edition, and Gayle Allen-Burket, Consultant in Chicago, Illinois, provided feedback on parts of the second edition. Farlee Wade Farber, Therapeutic Activities Coordinator, Special Care Unit, Washington Home and Hospice, Washington, DC, inspired many of the quality assurance concepts. William Parke, Administrator, and Pat Franklin, Director of Activities, and the activity staff of The Woodlands Skilled Nursing Facility in Rutherfordton, North Carolina, graciously cooperated in using the forms and completing a representative quality assurance study. Katharine Murphy, R.N., M.S., Gerontological Research Nurse Specialist, Hebrew Rehabilitation Center for Aged, contributed expertise regarding the federally mandated Resident Assessment Instrument. Mae Justice, Music Assistant, GreenTree Ridge, Asheville, North Carolina, has inspired the author's continued commitment to the value of activity pursuits throughout life and specifically the value of music in reaching beyond physical and cognitive deficits to the person who is still very much alive within. Mike Hopping, Medical Director for Blue Ridge Mental Health, Asheville, North Carolina, served as artist, reviewer, and consultant for both editions.

TABLE OF CONTENTS

1 INTRODUCTION

Activity programs cannot be copied or mass produced because their very success depends on innovation, creativity, and recognition of the individual. Each person has unique attributes that can be tapped through therapeutic activity programming. Seeking knowledge about how to better serve and understand each individual is a constant pursuit. This knowledge is the objective and the reward for every activity professional.

Activity pursuits play important roles in defining the meaning and satisfaction people experience throughout their lives. These pursuits are no less consequential in old age and, in fact, help human beings to negotiate the losses and challenges of frailty in a powerful and direct manner. This recognition provides a sound philosophical base for designing and implementing individualized activity programs.

Resident assessments are the first step in understanding individuals. Assessments viewed as mere paperwork miss the point at which the activity program can make real differences in individual lives. Residents' interactions with the activity program provide ongoing information about abilities, preferences, desires, dreams, aspirations, and hopes. Keen observations are necessary to the development of meaningful and effective resident assessments and lead to viable care plans.

Designing activity programs that have therapeutic value begins with understanding general resident functioning problems and needs. Once these commonalties are addressed, the program can focus on individual experiences. Applying adaptation to every group and individual activity facilitates the attainment of positive activity outcomes.

Each health professional's standards of practice require assessments, care planning, and program monitoring. The activity profession is unique in its focus on activity pursuits. Documentation of activity therapy assessments, care plans and program components furnishes a framework for care delivery, tools for quality assurance, and a system for communication. Written information about residents is needed to track outcomes and to plan the approach of each individual's care. It also illustrates the effectiveness of the overall program's design. A communication system ensures that resident care is coordinated and understood by others.

The activity profession is in its beginning developmental stages, and its purpose is often not understood by other professionals, family members, or residents. This book is written from the perspective of someone who has experienced this challenge. It is hoped that the reader will use this text as an opportunity for completing a successful journey through the vicissitudes and rigors held by this emerging profession.

The term "activity therapy" is used throughout the text and on the forms. It is not intended to refer to a prescriptive service that occurs for a limited amount of time. Instead, it is used with the belief that activity therapy is an aspect of all life and, for the frail elderly, it has particular value and meaning. The author views the activity program as a therapeutic device that reengages residents' interest in life by helping them realize dreams and aspirations. Therapeutic activities recognize residents' pain and struggles and provide an opportunity to heal this pain and cope with the aging process.

Activity pursuits serve a purpose throughout our lives. When our work is fulfilling, it focuses our energies on productive, rewarding activity. When we create art, we experience a part of ourselves that helps us touch the beauty of life. Activity therapy programs serve to remind residents of their purpose in life.

This book is not a comprehensive discussion of activity programs. It provides a point of view that encourages the activity professional to provide activity services tailored to every individual resident. The ideas presented here need to be adapted to individual settings, state and federal regulations, and individual residents. Understanding this individuality and how to adapt accordingly is at the crux of this material.

 **ACTIVITY PURSUITS**

The Meaning of Activity Pursuits Through the Life Span

Activity is the essence of life. It can be as mundane as brushing teeth or as exhilarating as reaching the top of a mountain. Our physical, social, and psychosocial well-being depends on activity. From childhood to death, we are engaged in pursuits that help us understand our world and give meaning to our existence. When life's activities are not in balance with life's needs, stress or boredom results. Extensive periods of this imbalance can lead to physical and emotional devastation, hopelessness, and eventually death.

Activity can be divided into two main categories. One is activities of daily living, and the other is activity pursuits. Activities of daily living (ADLs) are common daily tasks such as dressing, eating, and sleeping. We complete these tasks because they are necessary to staying physically healthy. Health provides the means for pursuing life's responsibilities and pleasures. Most of us do not think of brushing our teeth, getting dressed in the morning, or feeding ourselves as meaningful life activities. In fact, if we had no relationships, no responsibilities, and no challenges, we would soon lose interest in activities of daily living. What is the point of getting dressed if there is no place to go or no one to socialize with? ADLs alone do not enhance our well-being, but they give us a means for pursuing those activities which do add to the quality of our lives.

Activity pursuits refer to any activity outside of basic ADLs, that a person pursues to obtain a sense of well-being. Such activities benefit self-esteem, pleasure, comfort, health, education, creativity, success, and financial or emotional independence (Perschbacher, 1989). Activity pursuits cultivate meaningful relationships, sustain health, and foster optimal self-respect. Life without these activities is life stripped of individuality and even humanity.

Each individual's life is experienced through activity pursuits. Our beliefs and values are reflected in activity involvement patterns. For example, a lifelong farmer puts his personal beliefs into his farming practices. He believes in caring for nature, so he treats his farm with the best environmental techniques. He also believes in strong family ties, so he pursues farming practices that support his loved ones. Since both nature and family are important, he, at times, faces conflicting choices, such as: Should I pursue easy moneymaking farming methods or more expensive, environmentally-sound techniques?

Activity pursuits play a role in life from infancy to death. Those activities we pursue as children develop skills we use our entire lives. Children's social games teach relationship skills about competition, independence, and teamwork. Creative activities develop self-expression and artistic talents. Childhood activities help us to learn about our abilities, interests, and limitations. In adulthood, these skills are practiced in marriage, raising a family, and pursuing a career. As we enter later life, these skills are necessary for surmounting the losses intrinsic to aging, for understanding the failures and successes of the past, and for facing the inevitability of death.

Activity pursuits can be categorized into three types of activity experiences supportive, maintenance, and empowerment (Perschbacher, 1986). It is important to note that one specific activity event can support, maintain, and empower at the same time. These concepts should be viewed not as step-like but as fluid. The discussion here will focus on how these activity experiences apply generally throughout the life span. Chapter 8 will expand on how these experiences apply specifically to residents in long-term care.

Supportive Activity Experiences

Supportive activity experiences foster a sense of belonging. They include activities that recognize the significance of an individual's place in relationships with other people and with the environment. Relationships among human beings are nourished from the moment of birth. Family traditions are a prime illustration. In childhood, family life provides supportive experiences that develop the child's view of his/her place in the family. For example, many families' activities center around mealtimes. As a child sits at the table with other family members, an identity of self as part of the family unit begins to evolve. Thus, mealtime is a supportive activity the child uses to understand how he/she fits into the family structure. In adulthood, establishing one's own family reflects these childhood activities. As a father sits at the

table with his wife and children, mealtime again reinforces his identity in relation to his family. When an individual has grown up viewing the family togetherness at mealtime as a supportive activity, he/she may become distraught when this activity is changed by children who are not willing to join in daily family meals. In later life, if close family has been lost through death or distance, a person may seek to continue familiar supportive activities by entering a retirement center where meals are taken as a group.

Individuals facing significant losses use supportive activities to provide necessary solace. When a death occurs in a family, the family members frequently come together to comfort each other. This may happen through a variety of shared activities such as taking meals together, reminiscing, or playing traditional family games. As each activity takes place, family roles are played out. A grandmother may take charge to organize the meals. A grandson may provide entertainment for the younger children. As these activities and related roles unfold, children and adults alike will take comfort in knowing that, despite the loss of a loved one, they each retain a meaningful place in the family.

Supportive activities also provide respite in the face of overwhelming stress. For example, Gwen went to church with her grandparents as a child. During the hymns, her grandmother placed her arm around Gwen as they sang. This activity was a symbol of the love Gwen's grandmother felt for her granddaughter. As an adult, when Gwen is overwhelmed with her stressful job, she plays religious music. This gives her a sense of belonging by reminding her of the relationship with her grandmother. Her stress is momentarily forgotten, and she feels a sense of relief. In later life, Gwen is likely to use this same activity as a respite from stress.

EMPOWERMENT

MAINTENANCE

SUPPORTIVE

One's relationship with the environment is another important aspect of supportive activity experiences. Environment in this context refers to an individual's surroundings, including the environments created by nature and those created by human beings. The environment of nature reflects the path of human life. The consistency of the rising and setting sun is a constant reminder of one's existence and the passing of time. The growth and death of plant and animal life mirrors the cycle of each individual's own life. Much of this relationship with nature is developed through sensory experiences. A spring garden filled with flowers, vegetables, and insects can be experienced through touch, smell, taste, and hearing. Experiencing the environment gives one a sense of belonging to the earth. In later life, a relationship with the environment can evolve into a spiritual understanding of the reality of death.

To thrive in human society, man-made environments also must be understood. Learning to drive is an activity that facilitates a relationship with the environment. Developing skills in manipulating the environment provides a sense of confidence. This confidence reduces fear and promotes a sense of belonging to the human environment. In later life, such man-made environments can become difficult to negotiate due to sensory deficits. It becomes important to adapt the environment so that older individuals can continue to negotiate their surroundings as independently as possible.

Maintenance Activity Experiences

Maintenance activity experiences are pursued to maintain fitness. Maintenance activities promote physical functioning as well as cognitive and psychosocial health. ADLs are the mundane tasks of sustaining basic physical health. Maintenance activities go beyond these routine tasks and involve multiple choices about how health will be sustained. The ADL of eating involves the physical task of feeding oneself. However maintenance activities constitute eating choices as diverse as fixing a sandwich or a gourmet meal, eating out or eating at home.

Maintenance activity skills begin early in life. As children engage in physical sports and exercise programs, they develop a repertoire of physical maintenance activity skills. As one grows into adulthood, physical activities continue to promote fitness. An adult may have less time for sports activities but may find time to exercise a few minutes each day.

Relationship skills evolve as children participate in social activity experiences such as games, parties, and youth club projects. In adulthood, these social skills are carried into relationships with spouses, children, friends, and work cohorts. As a child, a young girl might participate in tea parties with favorite girlfriends. As an adult, this activity may become a weekly date for lunch with a special friend. Children who learn to get along with others during group activities are likely to maintain this skill in old age, even after many of their relationships have been lost.

Healthy emotional functioning is developed through participation in creative or expressive activity experiences. Children may use music, art, or writing to express sad or angry feelings. These skills can be used to cope with tragic losses or disappointments in adulthood.

Cognitive interests and abilities are discovered in childhood through participation in educational activities. This influences adult choices regarding a career and hobby pursuits. The child who excelled in history may choose a career in teaching or writing about history. If a career related to history is not feasible, he/she may join history clubs or read history books as a leisure pursuit.

Empowerment Activity Experiences

Empowerment activities go beyond simple maintenance of function by exceeding the required expectations and needs of daily life. In other words, empowerment activities stretch the limits of human potential. Since these activities are not mandatory, but are freely selected, individuals experience enriched choices and maximized control. Empowerment activities cultivate self-expression, increased responsibility, and personal challenges. They enhance self-respect because they are the peak expression of individualism.

Empowerment activities begin in childhood with activities that exceed the expected routines of daily functioning. A child may excel in sports beyond the basic participation requirements. A child may seek to study more than is expected in school. These activities may be sought because the child has discovered a strong interest or talent. A child who is musically gifted may exceed parent and teacher expectations by practicing beyond suggested requirements. A child who finds modern history interesting may surprise his/her parents by reading the newspaper rather than watching cartoons on television. Children who do not excel in school often will expend energy in other areas such as hobbies or sports.

Empowerment activities are pursued for the sake of the individual's experience of the activity. Though success in empowerment activities will often gain peer and adult recognition, this outcome is not the individual's motivation for participation. Self-respect through individual expression is the primary reward. Childhood achievements help eliminate the negative affects of peer and adult ridicule and prevent self-degradation.

Rather than supporting an individual's place within a community or family, empowerment activities promote an individual's ability to be different from others. Older adults who share oral history information with younger generations are participating in an empowering activity because it validates the significance of their individual experiences and knowledge. Empowerment plays a key role in the development of a positive self-concept.

Empowerment activities enjoyed as children influence adult activity choices. Adults with strong empowerment experiences as children may participate in volunteer work, exceed employment expectations and/or transcend basic leisure skills. For example, as a child, Tom was an outstanding student with multiple hobbies. He received many awards for meeting and exceeding educational requirements. However, his main interest was studying and collecting bones. As an adult, he became a successful lawyer. His interest in bones continued to be a main source of personal pleasure. He eventually wrote a book on the bone structure of wild animals in Wyoming. While this product was not a best seller, Tom's individual empowerment was fulfilled.

Recognizable Outcomes

Supportive, maintenance, and empowerment activities have recognizable outcomes for individuals. Individual needs and experiences will influence whether activity pursuits lead to positive outcomes. When activity pursuits are plentiful and successful, an individual's life will show beneficial results. If activity pursuits are limited and unsuccessful, a person's life will reflect the negative effects.

Supportive activities provide a positive validation of a person's relationship with the personal environment of family, friends, and nature. A person who experiences meaningful supportive activities will have a sense of belonging to his/her family, community, and the world at large. A person who does not experience meaningful supportive activities will not have a sense of belonging and will lack the skills to provide support to others.

Maintenance activities sustain maximal functioning with regard to health. An individual who participates in adequate maintenance activities will have good physical, cognitive, and psychosocial health. If adequate maintenance activities are not pursued, health will be compromised.

Empowerment activities promote peak individualism. A person who participates in empowerment activities is excited and challenged by the choices and possibilities of life. A person deprived of participation in this self-defining capacity will lack a sense of clear self-identity.

Individual differences with regard to needs and experiences influence how a person views a particular activity's benefits. A person who grew up on a farm may view gardening as a required activity that maintains physical health. A person who grew up in the city with few opportunities to watch plants grow may consider gardening an activity that provides self-satisfaction and empowerment. When a person's experience with a specific activity is unfavorable, he/she may view the activity as detrimental. A person who grew up in an abusive family situation may not experience mealtime as a positive, supportive activity. Instead, this person may identify his/her role in the family during mealtime as a catalyst for provoking abusive episodes.

The same activity can provide positive outcomes in all three areas. As mentioned earlier, a person can experience support, maintenance, and empowerment from one activity. Teresa learned cooking as a child. Cooking was not a family expectation, but something she chose as part of a 4-H project. In the cooking activity, she felt supported by her parents when they complimented the results; the food maintained her physical functioning; and she was empowered by learning this skill. As an adult, she and her husband had an annual Christmas party for their friends. This annual event was a supportive, maintenance, and empowerment experience. Teresa and her husband shared this activity and supported each other's abilities to provide an unforgettable Christmas event. Teresa maintained many social relationships by providing a social event for her friends. She also felt empowered by the event since the food was of excellent gourmet quality.

Activity pursuits help us define ourselves, validate our relationships, and maintain our health through action. The elderly have been engaged in this process since childhood. Now, as the losses and joys of old age surround their lives, activity pursuits offer opportunities to continue living as individuals with unique health and relationship needs.

Why Value Activity Pursuits in Long-Term Care?

Completion of ADLs is an accepted daily routine. Few human beings consider them a significant life accomplishment. Instead, they are a springboard for pursuing activities that give joy, require responsibility and challenge potential.

Unfortunately, when someone is admitted to a nursing home, restoring the ability to complete tasks of daily living often becomes the primary focus of caregiving. A review of most reimbursement systems and assessment tools shows an emphasis on ADLs while minimizing the role of activity pursuits. When older people become ill, it is unfair to assume they will be satisfied with something that alone is so unsatisfying. People want more and seek more every day.

Institutionalization does not change activity pursuit needs. Few human beings would bother to walk with the pain of a fractured hip if they had nowhere to go, no one to visit, and nothing of value to accomplish. Long-term care facilities need to focus on a balance of ADLs and activity pursuits reflective of normal human needs prior to institutionalization. This balance enhances residents' desire to successfully attend to

ADLs while continuing to lead a life filled with personal challenges, responsibilities, and successes.

Activity pursuits are not time fillers. They are the essence of who we are as individual human beings. As children, they provide lessons that apply to our adult accomplishments. Competition in sports shapes our desire and ability to compete on the job, for a partner, and for the best opportunities for our children. Playing with other children shapes our ability to work with others, dominate others, and/or negotiate with others as adults. Creative expression through participation in the arts shapes our ability to think creatively and develop solutions to difficult life problems. Adult opportunities for competition, play, and creativity stimulate us to change and grow into older adulthood.

As we age, we need a diverse collection of coping skills to deal with the inevitable physical, emotional, and social losses of growing old. We need to renew ourselves through continued pursuit of familiar activities and introductions to new pursuits. This renewal throughout old age heightens our competencies and gives us a reason to continue life. Being stripped of a multitude of activity pursuit opportunities dehumanizes our existence in a time when we need to understand the meaning of life before we die. Providing activity pursuit opportunities to the frail elderly is a societal obligation which assures that dignity is preserved and self-worth is valued.

3 BUILDING AN ASSESSMENT FOUNDATION

The goal of holistic assessment is to understand and document a specific individual's situation. The professional's ability to relate to this person augments the assessment's validity. Through relationships, the professional gains insight into behaviors, reactions, joys, and sorrows and recognizes changes when they occur. Paperwork must encompass this human factor by serving as a legitimate tool for finding solutions that mitigate problems and optimize quality of life. Humanizing the process of assessment is the most effective approach to achieving good outcomes.

Holistic assessment involves observing all aspects of a resident's life. This process then can be compared to the work of the detective who is constantly looking for clues in a complex and mysterious case. Observations, like clues, may not always suggest a clear cause. Disorientation can be the result of a recent stroke, dementia, and/or poor hearing. Variations in functioning, changes in relationships, and inconclusive observations make assessment an ongoing process throughout the resident's stay in a facility.

All assessments have essential and common components that establish a foundation for care planning and the achievement of positive results. This chapter will lay out basic assessment principles relevant to activity professionals as well as to other disciplines. Understanding these commonalties facilitates comprehensive interdisciplinary assessments and solution-oriented care plans.

Functioning, Characteristics, and Patterns

The initial phase of assessment consists of three areas: functioning, distinct resident characteristics, and comparisons of past and current patterns. As a baseline, assessments identify current physical, social, cognitive and emotional functioning levels. All areas of functioning are examined since they are interrelated and impact the results of any interventions. Each discipline's collection of information varies according to the scope of practice. Physical therapy assessments tend to emphasize mobility skills, and occupational therapy assessments focus on activities of daily living such as dressing and feeding one's self.

The second aspect of holistic assessment is the identification of distinct resident characteristics. These include interests, abilities, and customary routines. Characteristics shape perceptions and reactions to relationships and the environment. Comprehending their relevance is crucial to developing a partnership between the resident and the staff. Again, areas of emphasis vary according to the discipline. Nursing staff gather data about residents' habits such as preferred bathing times, while activity professionals concentrate on resident interests such as the specific type of music enjoyed.

In regard to functioning and individuality, assessments then compare the resident's past history with his/her current pattern. For example, the social services director compares past and current experiences with loss; the dietary director looks at past and current eating habits. These comparisons help professionals determine whether the resident's current patterns are related to a past lifestyle, a result of the current situation or a combination of both. This information forms the basis for setting expectations and approaches that are adapted to resident's unique life patterns.

Identification of functioning, resident characteristics, and current and past life patterns is the first step in completing assessments. This begins the relationship between the resident and facility staff. Once this information is obtained, it is analyzed to identify which facets relate to the potential outcome.

Determining Outcomes

Determining the type of outcome and when it will happen depends on a variety of factors. The impact of one area of functioning on another, strengths and weaknesses, length of illness, length of time in the facility and prognosis all are critical considerations. These common areas are a framework for instituting realistic time-oriented expectations and viable interventions.

COMMON FACTORS AFFECTING OUTCOMES

- **Impact of One Area of Functioning on Another**
- **Strengths and Weaknesses**
- **Length of Illness**
- **Length of Time in the Facility**
- **Prognosis**

Impact of One Area of Functioning On Another

One area of functioning is constantly interacting with another. A resident's feelings regarding loss can affect his/her motivation to participate in physical therapy. A deteriorating cognitive status can cause a person to withdraw from social relationships. The impact one area of functioning is having on another can be assessed by comparing recent changes in functioning with simultaneous life events. The past history is also used to ascertain what relationships exist. For example, a nursing home resident is suffering from a decline in physical status due to poor nutritional intake. This resident states that she has no interest in eating. Her assessment shows a close friend recently died. Her social record indicates a history of depression related to losses of family members and friends. The assessment process then leads staff members to focus on how her emotional status relates to her weakening physical status. A plan for addressing her feelings of grief is implemented and coordinated with a plan to increase her appetite. If the link between the emotional loss and the decrease in appetite had not been recognized, she would have been at risk for unnecessary physical and emotional deterioration. Recognizing the relationship of one area of functioning to another is crucial to attaining positive results.

Strengths and Weaknesses

Strengths and weaknesses influence expectations. Strengths are the balancing factor for how significantly weaknesses will affect recovery. Reviewing past lifestyle patterns is important to assessing a person's ability to deal with current difficulties. For example, two female residents are admitted to a facility with unstable fractured hips. Their medical histories are similar in that they both have arthritis with occasional severe pain but are otherwise in good physical health. One resident history indicates that she has coped successfully with a number of hardships in life. However, the second resident history shows a lifetime with relatively few hardships, but these difficulties have resulted in the resident becoming inactive and dependent on family members for long periods. The first resident is likely to participate actively and routinely in physical therapy interventions and recover rapidly. The second resident is likely to refuse physical therapy interventions or participate only with much encouragement. The recovery period is likely to be lengthier and possibly not as complete as the first resident's. In the case of the second resident, the staff can decrease the possibility for a negative outcome by anticipating the need for support and the possibility of a slower recovery.

Developing the care plan around an individual's strengths and weaknesses sometimes means the staff's expectations must be changed to match the resident's. Resident lifestyles have been set in place for a number of years. Taking this into consideration helps the staff negotiate with residents to identify realistic goals. For example, Mr. Sawyer is admitted with a diagnosis of diabetes. He is significantly overweight and has a high blood sugar. His history shows a lifelong tendency toward overeating. The director of dietary services would like for him to achieve an ideal body weight; however, Mr. Sawyer is not likely to completely change his eating pattern. Understanding this lifelong routine assists the staff to work with Mr. Sawyer in setting goals and approaches that accommodate his characteristics and maximize his compliance.

Length of Illness

Length of illness also influences the results that can be achieved over a given period of time. The longer a person suffers from an illness, the more debilitating it becomes. Inactivity, social deprivation, and emotional stress often accompany lengthy periods of frail health. These multiple difficulties require an extensive recovery period. For example, two residents are admitted to a facility following cerebrovascular accidents. The severity of the strokes is similar and both occurred on the left side. One resident, Ms. Mayfield, was inactive at home for a year before the stroke. This inactivity was due to a prior stroke, lack of motivation, and social isolation. The second resident, Ms. Johnson, was driving her car and taking an exercise class one week before the stroke. Ms. Johnson has a number of friends who visit her in the facility. Ms. Mayfield's recovery period will take longer than Ms. Johnson's due to her more extensive inactivity and lower personal expectations for recovery.

Length of Time in the Facility

The effect of time length in the facility on a resident bears careful consideration. Initial approaches to care are preliminary attempts to address needs based on a limited knowledge base. As the staff becomes increasingly familiar with a resident's preferences and responses, a more personal approach evolves. Dementia residents are particularly sensitive. For example, Ms. Bell is admitted to a facility with diagnoses of Alzheimer's disease, peripheral vascular disease, and chronic obstructive pulmonary disease. Her verbal and physical abusiveness is so severe that it interferes with the provision of daily care. Her initial outcome is poor. The staff are uncertain about how to work effectively with Ms. Bell because of her disorientation and abusive behavior. A variety of approaches are tried to determine what techniques get positive responses. As Ms. Bell interacts over a period of time with facility staff and the environment, valuable information is gained. In such a case, it can take four to six weeks of ongoing assessment to establish consistently viable approaches.

Prognosis

Prognosis is a necessary consideration in outcome determination. The severity and fluctuation of symptoms as well as the progression of the disease affect expectations. Ms. Bell's cognitive and physical status are expected to deteriorate. Symptoms of both may vary in severity daily or may change slowly over a long period of time. Care plan approaches may need to be changed throughout the day to adapt to variations in her functioning. In Ms. Bell's case, a good outcome might last only a few moments rather than several hours or days.

Participation in the Assessment and Care Plan

Examining functioning, characteristics and patterns, and their impact on outcomes provides a sound basis for making care delivery recommendations. These recommendations develop from the involvement of a number of parties. Family, friends, and staff members come together to broaden the assessment's scope and improve coordination of the care plan. This participation is important, but the resident's input is the critical factor in building an assessment foundation.

Resident Involvement

Residents making choices about their care becomes invaluable when it is an expected part of every interaction between staff members and residents. Currently, resident involvement is emerging as a routine practice. Resident input has been included in professional practice standards for a long time, but it only became a part of nursing home law with the passage of the Nursing Home Reform Section of the Omnibus Budget Reconciliation Act (OBRA) of 1987. Traditionally, nursing homes have used a medical model approach to care that emphasized the responsibility of the staff to care for a resident and de-emphasized the resident's ability to direct his/her care. Resident input was not actively sought. The nursing home reform law of 1987 moved nursing home care toward a wellness model approach, mandating resident participation in assessment and care planning. This approach assumes residents can take responsibility for their own care decisions.

The transition from a medical model to a wellness model requires alterations in routines and philosophical approaches. Initially, resident input is likely to be cursory. When residents attend care plan meetings, the staff may at first use this as a time to report to the resident what the staff has decided is best for him/her. As the evolution toward the wellness model occurs, staff members will become more adept at encouraging residents to define their own problems, goals, and approaches.

Resident involvement takes place in a variety of formats and should happen on a regular basis. Interviewing residents for the initial assessment and inviting them to a formal care plan meeting are two common examples. The initial assessment is an opportunity to acquaint the resident with the concept of making choices related to personal care as well as to other aspects of life in the facility. Some residents are able to identify preferences with direct, verbal statements that can be written into the assessment and care plan. However, other residents are unable to communicate verbally, so incorporating their choices into the process is done by observing behavior. A resident who suffers from dementia may not say, "I do not want to attend this activity." Instead, this resident may communicate dislike for an activity by leaving the room. An aphasic resident with a short attention span may show an interest in an event by sitting down and actively participating for a few minutes.

Formal care plan meetings usually involve an interdisciplinary team who designs goals and approaches. Attending this meeting can be an intimidating experience for anyone since it includes a number of people discussing personal matters related to care. Thus, a resident will feel more comfortable if he/she has been prepared in advance. This prepreparation includes explanations of the meeting's purpose, who will attend, and how long it will last. The resident is encouraged to express any reservations in advance and have the option to discuss matters in private beforehand. For example, a male resident who is having difficulties with incontinency may want to talk privately with a nurse and not have this issue addressed in the meeting.

A formal meeting is not always a viable option. When this happens, other alternatives merit exploration. Some residents are so intimidated by the meeting that they refuse to participate. For these residents, a one-on-one discussion with a key staff member may be more effective. Hosting care plan meetings with a smaller group of staff members in the resident's room is another possibility.

Residents who are disoriented or who make poor health care choices are unique challenges to the assessment process. Obviously a disoriented resident cannot take complete responsibility for making judgments related to care. However, many disoriented residents are capable of communicating problems such as incontinence, fear of falling and emotional stress. For example, Ms. Jaynes is a 75-year-old moderately disoriented resident. She wanders throughout the facility and is often heard saying, "I'm going crazy, it's so mixed up." As the day progresses, her wandering increases, and she becomes agitated and begins to stumble and fall. Here, Ms. Jaynes is demonstrating emotional stress verbally and through her agitated behavior. She is communicating physical stress by her unsteady gait and falls. The staff discovers that providing a structured routine of meaningful activity in the morning and assisting Ms. Jaynes to bed in the afternoon decreases her symptoms significantly. Her positive response to the staff's interventions illustrates their appropriateness.

Severely disoriented or comatose residents also can be included in the care process by reviewing personal histories and noting responses. These residents cannot communicate behavioral or verbal responses, thus leaving the staff unsure whether their approaches are suitable. In these situations, the staff have only the comprehensive assessment to rely on for making decisions. For example, Mr. Jones is a severely disoriented, 85-year-old resident whose wife and family visit daily. He currently suffers from low body weight and is at risk for skin breakdown. Mr. Jones was a farmer all his life. His customary routine had been to start his day at 5:00 a.m. by listening to the news. He then spent the day working in the fields. He ate lightly during the day and usually joined his wife for a large evening meal. His only known interests outside of work were spending time with his family, listening to religious music and watching game shows on television. Thus care plan approaches revolve around a routine of his past lifestyle. Activity pursuits include a radio in his room which is tuned to a news program in the early morning. Later in the morning, environmental tapes that reflect farming, e.g., hay blowing in the wind or rainstorms, or religious music are played. The television is tuned to game shows in the evening. The dietary department send him double portions of food for supper, and his wife usually assists with feeding him. Many of these approaches are implemented by his family because they visit daily and are familiar with his customary routine. While Mr. Jones cannot verbally tell the staff that his activity routine is appropriate, the assessment verifies the validity of using these approaches. If his food intake and body weight increase, the effect of large supper portions will be obvious.

Oriented residents who make poor health care choices present a situation that requires staff members to make a difficult compromise. Many health care professionals have a strong need to help others, and "helping," in a traditional medical model, means taking responsibility for resident decisions. Sometimes staff members feel frustrated when they cannot make appropriate choices for residents who appear to make detrimental decisions. A wellness model approach emphasizes staff members' ability to understand the personal nature of "appropriate" choices, i.e., what is appropriate for one person may not be for another, and prompts them to give up the desire to control resident behaviors. For example, a man who has never exercised routinely does not understand the benefits of participating in a daily exercise regime. The staff cannot make him participate in exercise so they educate him about the benefits he could gain. He agrees to exercise two times a week. The staff may not see this as the best health care choice, but it is a viable alternative.

Family Involvement

Family involvement is balanced with the resident's ability to provide information and to make decisions. Families provide an additional viewpoint for assessment information, especially with regard to the resident's history. Under a medical model, family participation in decision making often supersedes that of the resident; the resident's family is seen as the entity responsible for the resident's care. A wellness approach, however, looks to the family for decisions only in cases where the resident is unable to make those decisions.

Inviting the family to participate in the care plan meeting also involves education. The family needs to understand the purpose of the meeting, which family members will attend, how long the meeting will last, their role in assisting the resident, and when they need to make decisions. The family also should be encouraged to express any reservations in advance and have the option to discuss matters in private beforehand, e.g., family members who have questions regarding financial matters may prefer to discuss this topic only with the social worker.

Families are often an excellent asset in implementing the care plan. When a person enters a long-term care facility, family members sometimes feel their relationship no longer has the same value. In fact, family members can continue to have an important role in residents' lives. One way to assure them of the continuation of this role is to involve them in aspects of the care plan. Some examples include providing transportation to activities, bringing the resident's favorite foods, and asking friends who live in the community to visit.

Teamwork

Comprehensive resident assessments and viable care plans are dependent on the collaboration of an interdisciplinary team. This team shares information about assessment data and discipline-specific perspectives. This accumulation of data and viewpoints broadens the team's understanding of residents and provides multiple options for care planning.

Interdisciplinary teams have two main, interrelated tasks. The team's first task is to complete assessments and to design and implement care plans. The second task is to assure that the team effectively shares information and works together on behalf of the resident. If the importance of the second task is not recognized, much of the first task will be ineffective.

In nursing home facilities, a great deal of time is spent in care plan meetings. Relatively little of this time is delegated to assuring the team spends its time in a productive manner. The author has used team building as a method for helping care plan teams assess their efforts and implement approaches that maximize results. Team building uses all members of the team to identify problems, to create solutions, and to implement changes. This process is ongoing and includes an evaluation to assure that new strategies actually lead to resolutions. The process is unique to each team. Care plan teams might identify such problems as inefficient use of time, poor communication, and too much responsibility falling on one member or one discipline. *The Team Handbook: How to Use Teams to Improve Quality by Scholtes and others* (1988) is one of many excellent resources available on this subject. The team building process can lead to the achievement of well designed assessments and care plans, pleasant team relationships and coordinated implementation of approaches.

THE RESIDENT ASSESSMENT INSTRUMENT[1]

Overview

On December 22, 1987, Congress passed the Nursing Home Reform Section of the Omnibus Budget Reconciliation Act (OBRA). This legislation, commonly referred to as OBRA '87, represented the most dramatic legislative changes in nursing home regulation since the mid-70s. For the first time in federal nursing home law, quality of life was recognized as a key component of nursing home care. Previous regulations and laws had not specified this as a requirement or expectation. Congressional commitment that quality of life must become a reality was exemplified in the law's mandate that a federal nursing home resident assessment tool be developed.

Establishment of a federal assessment grew out of the findings of the Institute of Medicine's (IOM) Committee on Nursing Home Regulations which published its report Improving the Quality of Care in Nursing Homes in 1986. Outcomes of care, the value of assessment to the care planning process, facility management of quality care, and regulatory functions were established as important aspects of quality in nursing homes (Institute of Medicine, 1986). The IOM Committee noted that uniform resident assessment data could change the focus of the federal regulatory survey process and the care delivery system by shifting the emphasis from specific facility procedures to actual outcomes of care.

Development and Framework of the Resident Assessment Instrument

OBRA '87 required the Secretary of Health and Human Services to develop an assessment process. Under this legislative mandate, each nursing facility certified by Medicare and Medicaid must conduct a "comprehensive, accurate, standardized, reproducible assessment of each resident's functional capacities" (Omnibus Budget Reconciliation Act, 1987). This assessment is to describe the "resident's capability to perform daily life functions and significant impairments in functional capacity" and is to be based on a "uniform minimum data set" (Omnibus Budget Reconciliation Act, 1987). On February 2, 1989, the Secretary of Health and Human Services published the minimum data set in the Federal Register: "The comprehensive assessment must include at least the following information: medically defined conditions and prior medical history, medical status measurement, functional status, sensory and physical impairments, nutritional status and requirements, special treatments or procedures, psychosocial status, discharge potential, dental condition, activities potential, rehabilitation potential, cognitive status, and drug therapy" (Department of Health and Human Services, 1989).

The Health Care Financing Administration (HCFA), which establishes regulations for nursing homes, contracted with the Research Triangle Institute and its subcontractors, Hebrew Rehabilitation Center for Aged, Brown University, and the University of Michigan, to

---

1 Parts of this chapter were published in *Activities, Adaptation & Aging*, Volume 15, No. 4 1991.

develop and evaluate a resident assessment system. The assessment designed by this team is referred to as the Resident Assessment Instrument (RAI). Some individual states have chosen to use expanded versions of this instrument. These individual state assessments are acceptable by HCFA as long as they incorporate the RAI regulations established by the Secretary as well as any other requirements HCFA may institute. For a complete explanation of the RAI, the reader is encouraged to study the *Resident Assessment Instrument Training Manual and Resource Guide* (Morris, J. N., et al., 1991). This text will refer only to the RAI established by the Health Care Financing Administration and not to any individual state versions.

Extensive research, clinical review and revision were a part of the RAI's development. This tool's evolution was a participatory process. A number of individuals from a variety of disciplines including nursing, social work, geriatric and rehabilitative medicine, psychiatry, psychology, physical therapy, occupational therapy, speech therapy, activities, dietetics, and others were involved in its creation. Consumers, advocates, providers, regulators, researchers, and experts in measurement also took part in this project.

The Research Triangle team with the input of these other experts developed a resident assessment tool consisting of two parts: the Minimum Data Set for Nursing Home Resident Assessment and Care Screening (MDS) and the Resident Assessment Protocols (RAPs). The MDS is based on the areas the Secretary specified and is designed to capture the "minimum" information needed to begin a comprehensive assessment. The MDS recognizes the resident as an individual with diverse physical, emotional, and social needs. While many aspects of the MDS focus on the functional status of the resident, other items deal with individual preferences such as customary routines and activities. The MDS takes a holistic view of individual residents and assists in identification of how a resident's strengths and needs in one area affect other areas of his/her life (Morris, J. N., et

al., 1990). The MDS can be found in Appendix A. The reader is encouraged to make a copy and use it as a reference throughout this book.

Resident Assessment Protocols (RAPs) consist of "triggers" and related "guidelines". The RAPs are linked to the MDS by "triggers" or red flags consisting of one or more particular MDS items. The "triggers" identify actual or potential problems. The "guidelines" provide a framework for in-depth assessment in specific problem areas. For example, if the MDS indicates that a resident has fallen in the last thirty days, the Falls RAP will be "triggered". The RAP Guidelines will enable the assessor(s) to identify the underlying problem that may have caused the fall, e.g., hypotension as a side effect of medication, and therefore suggest approaches that can alleviate future fall risks.

The following eighteen areas make up the RAPs in the RAI: delirium, visual function, ADL functional/rehabilitation potential, psychosocial well-being, behavior problem, falls, feeding tubes, dental care, psychotropic drug use, cognitive loss/dementia, communication, urinary incontinence/catheter, mood state, activities, nutritional status, dehydration/fluid maintenance, pressure ulcers, and physical restraints. Each of these RAPs has information relevant to activity assessment and care planning. This book will focus primarily on the Activities RAP. The reader should also study the content of the other RAPs to discover their interrelationships to activity programming.

Each RAP contains a description of the condition or problem, the specific "triggers" linking it to the MDS, the "guidelines" for further assessment and a summary page called the RAP Key (page 126). Referring to the Activities RAP in Appendix B, the reader should note that under Section I (Problem) is a description of the key characteristics of activities and why it is important to consider this area for nursing home residents. Section II ("triggers") identifies the MDS Triggers that relate to the resident's potential activity problems or needs. Section III ("guidelines") presents ideas for evaluating the "triggered" activity condition. These "guidelines" facilitate an assessment of factors that may cause or contribute to the Activities' "triggers". At the end of the Activities RAP is the

RAP Key, a quick reference that summarizes the Activities RAP. The "triggers'" section of the RAP Key lists each of the four activities "triggers". The "guidelines'" section of the RAP Key briefly indicates other relevant MDS items (Morris, J. N., et al., 1991).

The RAI training manual and the federal regulations for nursing homes list a number of requirements related to the RAI. This text will summarize the RAI process as it relates to completion procedures, information sources, schedule of assessments, coding, and time frames; however, these materials are not intended to provide a comprehensive understanding of the RAI. This can be achieved only by a thorough study of both the manual and the regulations. The federal regulations are often subject to change and the reader will need to stay abreast of any modifications that are made over time to the RAI.

The regulations require an RN to coordinate the RAI process with the input of other appropriate health professionals. The RN coordinator is required to sign and certify completion of the MDS. Other individuals who fill in any part of the MDS must sign and indicate which section(s) they completed. Each professional is responsible for the accuracy of the section(s) he/she completes. Other procedures for this coordination are not dictated. Some facilities assign specific disciplines to fill in particular sections of the MDS. Other facilities may have an RN complete all the MDS items.

In the text's discussion of MDS Section I, the author assumes that completion is done by the activity professional. Whether or not the actual items are filled in by the activity professional, he/she should be responsible for providing input into Section I. Other sections may also be completed by the activity professional according to his/her assessment skills and a given facility's procedures.

The person(s) completing the MDS consults the medical record as well as the interdisciplinary team (including the physician), the family, the nursing staff (including nursing assistants) and the resident. A record review is a necessary initial step in completing the MDS. This review will provide each discipline's current perspective of the resident as well as historical information. The written record contains data across shifts and over multiple days. For residents who have been in the facility for a long time, functioning patterns are revealed through monthly summaries, test results, progress notes, etc.

Consulting with multiple resources regarding the resident's condition will assure a more complete and accurate picture. For example, the first item of Section I (Figure 4.1) assesses the amount of time a resident is awake. Morning and evening shift nurses, nursing assistants, family members, rehab professionals, and the resident all may have information related to this item. When input includes a broad spectrum of resources, the MDS items are more likely to reflect the resident's actual status.

The assessment schedule varies according to each individual resident's situation. Initial assessments for new residents must be completed by the 14th day of residency. These may be updated through day 21 if changes in resident status occur or new information becomes available. An annual reassessment is required every twelve months. When a resident experiences a significant change, he/she is to be assessed within fourteen days of the occurrence of the change. Quarterly reviews include selected parts of the MDS, i.e., cognitive patterns, communication/hearing ability, physical functioning and ADL abilities, continence, mood and behavior patterns, new disease diagnoses, weight loss, medication use, and special treatments and procedures. These reviews are completed every three months and are done during the same time period as quarterly progress notes and care plans.

The MDS uses coding conventions that must be followed. (Refer to your copy of the MDS or Appendix A.)

1. Each section of the MDS has one or more items labeled sequentially, e.g., the third item in Section I is I.3.
2. A check mark is used for the clear white boxes (no shading) if the condition is met. If it is not met, these boxes remain blank. For lightly shaded boxes, a numeric response is used. The darker shaded areas remain blank.

3. When an ordered set of responses is used, e.g., independent to dependent, zero ("0") is used to indicate the lack of a problem. Refer to Section E, Physical Functioning and Structural Problems. Note the use of "0" in items E3 and E6.

4. Printed capital letters are used in any open-ended response such as "occupation," e.g., CARPENTER.

5. When information is not available, it is coded with an "NA." The responses "None of the Above" is only checked when the other responses do not apply and should not be checked to indicate the information is not available.

6. There are a few instances when the MDS instructions require you to skip items, e.g., when you answer "1" for Section B1, you then go directly to Section E.

Each item of the MDS refers to specific time frames. Seven days is the most common time frame. Others include three days, fourteen days, thirty days, ninety days, one hundred eighty days, and one year. To assure all staff members are referring to a uniform period of time, Section A1 provides a space to document the assessment date. This date is a specific point in time and all MDS items refer back in

---

Figure 4.1
Section I. Activity Pursuit Patterns

1.	**TIME AWAKE**	(*Check appropriate time periods* over last 7 days) Resident awake all or most of time (i.e., naps no more than one hour per time period) in the: Morning a. Evening c. Afternoon b. NONE OF ABOVE d.
2.	**AVERAGE TIME INVOLVED IN ACTIVITIES**	0. Most--More than 2/3 of time 2. Little--less than 1/3 of time 1. Some--1/3 to 2/3 of time 3. None
3.	**PREFERRED ACTIVITY SETTINGS**	(*Check all settings* in which activities are preferred) Own room a. Outside facility d. Day/activity room b. NONE OF ABOVE e. Inside NH/off unit c.
4.	**GENERAL ACTIVITIES PREFERENCES (adapted to resident's current abilities)**	(*Check all PREFERENCES* whether or not activity is currently available to resident) Cards/other games a. Spiritual/religious activities f. Crafts/arts b. Trips/shopping g. Exercise/sports c. Walking/wheeling outdoors h. Music d. Watch TV i. Read/write e. NONE OF ABOVE j.
5.	**PREFERS MORE OR DIFFERENT ACTIVITIES**	Resident expresses/indicates preference for other activities/choices 0. No 1. Yes

time from this date. If for example, the assessment date is May 14th, the items with seven day time frames would refer to May 7th to May 14th.

Overview of the RAI's Relation to Activities

"Activity potential" was listed in the February 2, 1989, Federal Register as one of the required components of the MDS. Activity potential was defined in the HCFA State Operations Manual (Department of Health and Human Services, 1992) as "the resident's ability and desire to take part in activities which maintain or improve physical, mental, and psychosocial well-being. Activity pursuits refer to any activity outside of Activities of Daily Living (ADLs) which a person pursues in order to obtain a sense of well-being. [This] also includes activities which provide benefits in self-esteem, pleasure, comfort, health, education, creativity, success, and financial or emotional independence.[2] The assessment should consider the resident's normal everyday routines and lifetime preferences." This definition of activity potential is a framework for establishing activity assessments and care planning.

All aspects of the MDS are relevant to the activity assessment. Some areas are more specific to activity pursuits than others. The most relevant MDS Section is entitled "Activity Pursuit Patterns" (Figure 4.1). This section assesses the interrelationship between the resident's time awake and his/her average time involvement in activity pursuits. It also looks at activity preferences with regard to where a resident prefers to participate, general types of activities a resident is interested in, and whether a resident desires more or different choices with regard to activities.

---

2. This description of activity pursuits originated from position papers written by the author for the National Association of Activity Professionals from 1986-1990 and was introduced in Chapter 2.

MDS Section I has five items. The first item (1) focuses on the amount of time the resident is awake during the morning, afternoon and evening. The second item (2) identifies the resident's average time involvement in activities as most, some, little, or none. The third item (3) lists four preferred activity settings: own room, day/activity room, inside nursing home/off unit, and/or outside facility. The fourth item (4) has a listing of general activity preferences adapted according to the resident's current abilities. These preferences are: cards/other games, crafts/arts, exercise/sports, music, reading/ writing, spiritual/religious activities, trips/shopping, walking/wheeling outdoors, and/or watching TV. The fifth item (5) indicates a resident's preference for more or different activities.

Accurate completion of the MDS requires the assessor to have an understanding of the item-by-item instructions before any coding is done. This understanding includes intent, definitions, process and coding information. For this reason, the instructions for Section I are included immediately below.

Section I
Activity Pursuit Patterns

Intent: To determine the amount and types of interests and activities that the resident currently pursues, as well as activities the resident would like to pursue that are not currently available.

Definition: **Activity pursuits** refer to any activity other than ADLs that a person pursues to enhance a sense of well-being; these pursuits include activities that provide increased self-esteem, pleasure, comfort, education, creativity, success, and financial or emotional independence.

1. **TIME AWAKE**

Intent: To identify those periods of a typical day (over the last seven days) when resident was awake all or most of the time (i.e., no more than one hour nap during any such period).

Process: Consult with caregivers, resident, and family members.

Coding: Check all periods when resident was awake all or most of the time. **Morning** is from 7 a.m. (or when resident wakes up, if later) until noon; **afternoon** is from noon to 5 p.m.; **evening** is from 5 p.m. to 10 p.m. (or bedtime if earlier).

2. **AVERAGE TIME INVOLVED IN ACTIVITIES**

Intent: To determine the proportion of available time that resident was involved in activity pursuits as an indication of overall activity-involvement pattern; refers to time when resident could have been involved in activity pursuits (awake and not receiving treatments or support with ADLs).

Process: Consult with caregiver, activities staff members, resident, and family members. Ask about time involved in different activity pursuits.

Coding: In coding this item, exclude time spent in receiving treatments (e.g., medications, heat treatments, changing bandages, rehabilitation therapies, or ADLs).

Include time spent in pursuing independent activities (e.g., watering plants, reading, letter-writing; social contacts with family, residents, staff, and volunteers; activity pursuits in a group or on a one-on-one or individual basis).

3. **PREFERRED ACTIVITY SETTINGS**

Intent: To determine activity circumstances/settings that the resident prefers including (though not limited to) circumstances in which resident is at ease.

Process: Ask resident, family, caregiver, and activities staff about resident's preferences. Knowledge about observed behavior can be helpful, but it only provides part of the answer. **Do not limit preference list to areas to which the resident now has access.**

Coding: Check all responses that apply. If the resident does not wish to be in any of these settings, check **NONE OF ABOVE.**

4. **GENERAL ACTIVITIES PREFERENCES (ADAPTED TO RESIDENT'S CURRENT ABILITIES)**

Intent: To determine which activities, of those in the selected list, the resident would prefer to participate in (independently or with others). **Choice is not limited by whether or not the activity is currently available to the resident, or whether the resident currently engages in the activity.**

Definition: **Exercise/sports**—Includes any type of physical activity (e.g., dancing, training, weight, sports).

Spiritual/religious activities —Includes participating in religious services as well as watching them on television or listening to them on the radio.

Process: Consult with resident, resident's family (if present), activities staff members, and nursing assistants. Explain that activity pursuits are adaptable to resident's ability. For example, when asking a resident about his/her preference for reading, explain availability of taped books or large print if the resident is unable to read small print.

Coding: Check for each activity preferred. If none are preferred, check **NONE OF ABOVE**.

5. **PREFERS MORE OR DIFFERENT ACTIVITIES**

Intent: To determine if resident expressed interest in pursuing activities **NOT** offered at the facility (or on the residential unit). **This includes situations in which the activity is provided but the resident would like to have other choices in carrying out the activity** (e.g., the resident would like to watch news on TV rather than the game shows and soap operas preferred by the majority of residents; or the resident would like a Methodist Church service rather than the Baptist service scheduled for most residents).

Residents who resist attendance/involvement in activities offered at the facility also are included in this category (to determine possible reasons for lack of involvement).

Process: Ask resident if there are things he/she would enjoy doing (or used to enjoy doing) that are not currently available or, if available, are not "right" for him/her in their current format. If the resident is unable to answer, ask the same question of a close family member, friend (if available), activity professional, or nursing assistant.

Coding: Choose only one response.

(Morris, J. N., et al., 1991)

It was established in Chapter 2 that activity pursuits are an essential part of every person's life. For this reason, every resident in a nursing home merits a plan of care that identifies activity pursuit needs and goals. Each item in the MDS Section I provides useful information about activity pursuit patterns whether or not it leads to a "triggered" condition. Figure 4.2 (page 25) is based on the case example of Ms. Smith. She will be briefly introduced in this chapter as her case relates to MDS Section I and will be given more attention in Chapter 6 as a case example for completing the comprehensive activity assessment. Initially her case will be used to illustrate the value of each MDS section item without considering the Activities Trigger Conditions.

Ms. Smith

Ms. Smith is a 77-year-old woman who is admitted to a rehab unit after suffering a severe stroke. During her stay, she participates fully in rehabilitation therapy. Speech, occupational and physical therapy are discontinued when it is determined that she has reached her maximum potential.

Ms. Smith is transferred to a long-term care facility. At admission, she has complete paralysis of her right side, loss of most of her speech, and an inability to ambulate independently. Ms. Smith's orientation is unaffected by the stroke. She uses gestures, "yes/no" responses, and hand movements to indicate her needs. She is withdrawn and dependent on staff members for tasks she is capable of performing herself. She tries to get the nursing staff to pour water into her mouth when she takes her medicine rather than holding the cup for herself. Ms. Smith appears to not trust the staff while they assist her with showers. She is capable of learning to propel her own wheelchair but refuses to attempt this. She rings her call bell several times during each shift. When the nursing assistants answer, her requests are often for something she can do for herself. Ms. Smith's limited communication skills are a constant frustration to her as evidenced in her facial expressions. She refuses to attend any group activities, not even gospel music activities which her assessment indicates is a past interest.

Ms. Smith's previous lifestyle included many diverse interests, most of which she engaged in until her stroke. She was an active member of the community and her church. Ms. Smith's careers included being a homemaker, a school teacher and a professional singer. She enjoys children and takes pride in her musical abilities. She raised a family of three boys and one girl and is proud of their accomplishments. Her husband died several years ago, and her daughter reports that she coped well with his death. Her family is supportive but are only able to visit one time weekly. She sometimes cries when she is asked about her past lifestyle.

Ms. Smith forms a positive relationship with one nursing assistant, Deanna. Even though she can only say a few words, Ms. Smith still sings the words to familiar songs. Deanna and Ms. Smith often sing while Ms. Smith's morning care is being done.

MDS Section I (Figure 4.2) identifies Ms. Smith's time awake (Item 1) and the average time she spends involved in activity pursuits (Item 2). Understanding the interrelationship of these items pinpoints positive activity outcomes or potential negative outcomes. The amount of time awake, the time available for activity pursuits and the actual amount of time spent in activity involvement depicts an important aspect of a resident's activity pursuit pattern. A resident who is awake much of the day (Item 1a, b, and c checked), and spends minimal time in ADLs and treatments obviously has a great deal of time available. If this same resident is shown to actually have little or no involvement in activities (Item 2, Code 2 or 3), he/she is passing a considerable period without being engaged in meaningful activity. This is the situation with Ms. Smith. This limited participation pattern can lead to boredom, agitation or withdrawal and can have a profoundly negative effect on physical health.

It was discussed earlier that assessing the amount of time a resident is awake (Figure 4.2, Item 1) requires consultation with several sources, i.e., morning and evening shifts, rehabilitation professionals, family, resident, etc. The activity professional may want to develop a form to document this information and/or use interviews. Chapter 9 shows how activity participation records can be used to document residents' reasons for lack of attendance including being asleep. Once a clear pattern of time awake is established, activities of interest to the resident can be scheduled accordingly.

Assessment of involvement (Figure 4.2, Item 2) encompasses a broad definition of activity pursuits. The reader should pay special attention to the coding definition for Section I-Item 2 (page 22). Involvement embodies the resident's participation in structured group and individual activity programs **as well as** independent activities. Unfortunately, this latter area is sometimes not taken into consideration since it is not part of professional services. Residents who spend much of their time in autonomous pursuits are engaged in meaningful activities whether or not this occurs as part of a formal program. An accurate picture of activity pursuit patterns is not possible without including the entire scope of resident participation. In Ms. Smith's case, the activity professional considers Ms. Smith's lack of attendance to facility programs as well as her participation in independent activities such as family visits and singing with Deanna in her room. This combination of factors, along with the amount of time she has available for activity pursuits, determines the average time involvement to be coded.

MDS Section I-Item 3 indicates the location where a resident wants to participate. Residents who have many preferences show positive outcome potential, while residents who have few preferences are at risk for a poor outcome. Limited setting preferences reduce the resident's access to activity choices. The activity professional needs to design approaches that compensate for this. For example, Ms.

Figure 4.2
Section I. Activity Pursuit Patterns: Ms. Smith's Initial MDS

1.	TIME AWAKE	(*Check appropriate time periods* over last 7 days) Resident awake all or most of time (i.e., naps no more than one hour per time period) in the:	
		Morning a. ✓ Evening c. ✓	
		Afternoon b. ✓ NONE OF ABOVE d.	
2.	AVERAGE TIME INVOLVED IN ACTIVITIES	0. Most--More than 2/3 of time 2. Little--less than 1/3 of time 1. Some--1/3 to 2/3 of time 3. None	
3.	PREFERRED ACTIVITY SETTINGS	(*Check all settings* in which activities are preferred) Own room a. ✓ Outside facility d. Day/activity room b. NONE OF ABOVE e. Inside NH/off unit c.	
4.	GENERAL ACTIVITIES PREFERENCES (adapted to resident's current abilities)	(*Check all PREFERENCES* whether or not activity is currently available to resident) Cards/other games a. Spiritual/religious activities f. ✓ Crafts/arts b. Trips/shopping g. Exercise/sports c. Walking/wheeling outdoors h. Music d. ✓ Watch TV i. ✓ Read/write e. NONE OF ABOVE j.	
5.	PREFERS MORE OR DIFFERENT ACTIVITIES	Resident expresses/indicates preference for other activities/choices 0. No 1. Yes	1.

Smith states she enjoys participating in music programs but prefers to stay in her room. Because of this choice, she has formed few close relationships. A gospel music activity is scheduled in the facility and will be held in the dining room. The activity professional educates her about this opportunity and provides supportive approaches such as inviting Deanna, her nursing assistant, to attend the event with her to increase her comfort level. If Ms. Smith still prefers to stay in her room, it may be possible to video tape the event and have her view it in her room.

MDS Section I-Item 4 represents general activity preferences over the last seven days. The resident only needs to communicate an interest in these activities regardless of actual participation in them. Many residents who are new admissions have been recently hospitalized and have not had access or energy to participate in activities. Explaining that activities can be adapted for the resident's current functioning status elicits a more complete description of actual interests. For example, a resident who has played cards in the past may not be familiar with card holders or large print cards and may not list it as a current preference because he/she may assume it will require abilities, i.e., good dexterity and eyesight, that he/she does not have. In completing Ms. Smith's MDS, the activity professional explains how each activity can be adapted to Ms. Smith's abilities and deficits, e.g., Ms. Smith is told that wheelchair transportation will be provided to and from activities of her choice, i.e., music and religious activities.

Section I-Item 5 uncovers a desire for more or different activity choices **and/or** lack of involvement in the structured activity program. Looking at MDS Section I, and not the item instructions, would leave the impression that Item 5 only identifies residents who have expressed a desire for different activity choices. Review the MDS item-by-item instructions again under Item 5 (page 23). This reveals the additional focus on residents who do not involve themselves in the facility's programs. This section assumes that lack of participation in the structured activity program usually reflects a desire for different activity choices. A resident who chronically refuses to attend activities merits a review to determine the reason. Further investigation may show that the resident participates in numerous independent activities. For many residents, further review substantiates other issues, such as lack of specific activity choices the resident can identify with or lack of access to activity programs of choice, e.g., resident is in bed during preferred activities or has low self-esteem due to perceived inabilities. Ms. Smith's comprehensive activity assessment in Chapter 6 will show that several of these issues are affecting her participation in the structured program.

The above explanation of Ms. Smith's case illustrates the value of Section I to an assessment of an individual's activity pursuit pattern without considering whether the items are "triggers". This is an important concept since every resident needs to maintain an activity pursuit pattern and requires an activity care plan. If a resident is not "triggered" in a particular area, the MDS data continues to have value to the common need for activity care planning.

Figure 4.3, Activities Triggers (page 27) targets four specific conditions that can profoundly affect resident involvement patterns. These "triggers" use MDS items from Section 1, Activity Pursuit Patterns alone or in combination with items from other sections to "trigger" a need for specialized activity care planning. Particular activity patterns that are potentially unsatisfying or unsafe are identified. The previous discussion of Ms. Smith's case focused on the relevance of Section I to common activity needs. The following discussion will show how her case is pertinent to the conditions of "triggers" 1 and 2 . Other case examples will be used to discuss "triggers" 3 and 4.

Activity Trigger 1 identifies a resident who prefers more or different activity choices. Many residents "trigger" under this item because of their request(s) for different types of activity choices. In the prior discussion of Ms. Smith's case, it was noted that the coding explanation also includes the resident's lack of participation in the structured activity program. Ms. Smith is coded 1 under Section I, Item 5 because of her lack of attendance at activity programs. This activities "trigger" provides a starting point for determining why the resident is expressing a need for different activity choices and/or is not involved in the structured activity program.

Activity Trigger 2 describes a resident who has little involvement in activities, is experiencing distress, and has communication and/or cognitive abilities. This resident condition is "triggered" by a combination of items from Section I as well as Sections G (psychosocial well-being), H (mood and behavior patterns), B (cognitive patterns), and C (communication/hearing patterns). Compare each of these items to the full MDS form (Appendix A). A resident who is experiencing emotional difficulty and limited activity involvement is targeted since distress can be decreased or eliminated with increased participation in activity pursuits. The resident's communication and/or cognitive abilities suggest that the resident has the

Figure 4.3
Activities Triggers

II. TRIGGERS

The following sets of MDS based conditions indicate those residents who will require further review, as well as the types of action that may be required:

1. Revised activity plan suggested if:

   Resident Prefers More or Different Activity choices **[I5 = 1]**

2. Revised activity care plan suggested to help resident overcome resident distress when ALL THREE of the following conditions met:
   a. *Little/No* involvement in activities **[I2 = 2 or 3]**
   b. *One/More* of following indicators of Distress:
      - Unsettled relationships in any area **[G2a, G2b, G2c, G2d = Any checked]**
      - Sadness over lost roles/status **[G3b = checked]**
      - Verbal expressions of sad mood **[H1a = checked]**
      - Withdrawn — as indicated by complete absence of General Activity Preferences **[I4] = checked]**

   c. Two or more of following indicators of Communication/Cognitive Ability:
      - Short-term memory OK **[B2a = 0]**
      - At least some decision-making ability **[B4 = 0, 1, or 2]**
      - Understood/usually understood by others **[C4 = 0 or 1]**
      - Understood/usually understands others **[C5 = 0 or 1]**

3. Review of activity care plan to determine if its modification might help to overcome resident distress when either of the following conditions met:
      - -a- and -b- conditions above AND resident is bedfast **[E4b = checked]**
      - -a- and -b- conditions above AND resident has *No or Only One* of the four indicators of Communication/Cognitive ability (c. above).

4. Review of activity care plan suggested if: Most involvement in activities **[I2 = 0]** *AND* Two or more checked in measurement of time awake **[I1a, I1b, I1c = more than 1 checked]**

capacity to participate in activities successfully and other reasons for nonparticipation need to be assessed. Ms. Smith's Section I, Item 2 (Figure 4.2) shows she has little involvement in activities. Her case study indicates she has unsettled relationships and sadness over lost roles/status (Section G.). Her cognitive and communication abilities include a good short term memory (Section B), decision-making skills (Section B), and an ability to understand others (Section C). Her condition requires in-depth activity care planning since she has a wide scope of emotional and physical problems compounded by poor activity participation. Her communication and cognitive abilities are assets to developing the care plan.

Compare "triggers" 2 and 3 above. Both focus on little involvement in activities and distress. "Trigger" 3 includes a resident who is bedfast or who has severely impaired communication and/or cognitive abilities. A resident who is bedfast, distressed and has little involvement in activities certainly merits special attention. For example, Ms. McGuire has extremely limited physical endurance secondary to a rapidly progressing cancer. She is in bed throughout the day and rarely participates in activities. She frequently becomes angry at the staff and is tearful during many of her conversations. A review of her activity care plan needs to be done to assess how her distress can be decreased. Increased activity participation can address the emotional stress and isolation inherent in being bedfast.

The other type of resident in "trigger" 3 has severe communication and/or cognitive deficits. For example, Mr. Gustafson rarely participates in activities, expresses fear about his environment, and has poor memory and limited decision-making activities. His situation requires a revised activity care plan that adapts activities to his cognitive deficits while reducing his stress level.

Activities Trigger 4 identifies a resident who is awake much of the day and is involved in activity pursuits most of the time. Further evaluation of this type of resident is necessary to determine whether he/she is overextending him/herself physically. For example, Mr. Garland is a resident who is involved in group and individual activities several hours each day. He particularly enjoys participating in exercise and sports activities. During the past few weeks, he has begun to complain of shortness of breath and has appeared pale and at times lethargic. The activity professional and nursing staff are concerned that he may not be taking enough rest periods. An assessment of his physical status is initiated to ascertain whether he needs to limit his activity participation.

Once the "triggered" conditions are identified, the RAI process moves to the RAPs Guidelines. The MDS and the "triggers" must be followed according to federal regulations; however, the RAP Guidelines provide a direction for assessments and care planning without being prescriptive. This leaves room for flexibility, a necessary component of individualized programming.

The Activities RAP Guidelines (Appendix B) direct the activity professional to review a variety of areas which might affect a resident's involvement in activities. When one of the four "trigger" conditions has been identified, these "guidelines" provide insight into further assessment areas. They also can be helpful in designing an activity assessment tool for use with all residents. The activity assessment form in Chapter 6 will illustrate many of these "guidelines" as well as the progress note form in Chapter 9. The Activities RAP examines the following questions:

1. Is the resident suitably challenged or over-stimulated?

2. What health-related factors may be affecting activity participation?

3. Has the resident experienced a recent decline in functioning?

4. Are there environmental factors which could impact activity involvement?

5. Have there been any changes in availability of family, friends, or staff support?

6. Are there confounding problems to be considered for those now activity involved in activities?

Under each question, the Activities RAP provides further information and questions. In Mr. Garland's situation, (activities "trigger" number four), exploring the last question "Are there confounding problems to be considered for those now actively involved in activities?", helps the staff decide if he is overextending his physical endurance limitations

It was noted earlier that the activities "triggers" make connections with several other areas of the MDS, i.e., G (Psychosocial Well-being), H (Mood and Behavior Patterns), B (Cognitive Patterns), and C (Communication/Hearing Patterns), E (Physical Functioning and Structural Problems. The Activities RAP Guidelines also lead the activity professional to other areas of the MDS and/or other RAPs. For example, the activities RAP question "Is the resident suitably challenged or over stimulated?" could be answered in part by reviewing MDS Sections I, II, and III. This background information is collected only at admission. It includes such items as birth date, lifetime occupation, marital status and customary routines. Section III, Customary Routine, is of particular value. A picture of the resident's daily life patterns before entering the long term care facility is presented. Data about resident preferences with regard to use of time, for example, "stays busy with hobbies, reading or fixed daily routine," and "stays up late at night" provide clues for scheduling group or individual activities. If the resident is in the habit of staying busy until late in the evening and now has a limited activity involvement pattern, he/she may not be "suitably challenged."

Chapter 3 describes the value of interrelationships between functioning areas and how these relate to making an appropriate intervention. The MDS, "triggers" and RAPs maximize this principal by constantly interrelating one item to another. Chapter 6 provides a more comprehensive view of how multiple MDS sections affect activity pursuit patterns.

Summary

The RAI is a format for cultivating resident outcomes by understanding the diversity and uniqueness of each nursing home resident. Recognition of the potential of this assessment tool will assure that the congressional desire for quality of life will be realized. The focus of this assessment must remain on improving the lives of nursing home residents. Participating in this new challenge presents a felicitous opportunity to illustrate the impact of activities on positive resident outcomes.

MDS Section I gives some basic activity pursuit pattern information and identifies four specific resident conditions. The RAPs ask questions related to the "triggered" conditions. The RAI process is a useful beginning step in the activity assessment process. Integrating Section I, the other sections of MDS and the RAPs with an activity assessment that is based on standards of practice is the next step in building an effective care planning foundation.

 **STANDARDS OF PRACTICE FOR ACTIVITY PROFESSIONALS**

Standards of Practice are the foundation for professional services. They cover a wide variety of practices including ethics, objectives, and documentation. Those most germane to this text are standards that address activity assessment, care planning, and programming.

Several activity therapy disciplines have standards. Music therapists, recreation therapists, and art therapists are among the most obvious. These standards are, however, limited to one aspect of activity, i.e., music, recreation, and art, and they address the needs of diverse populations, e.g., developmentally disabled, elderly, and mentally ill. The standards of the National Association of Activity Professionals (NAAP) pertain specifically to diverse activity programs for primarily geriatric populations. The reader can find these in Appendix C. They will be briefly summarized here and will be referred to in other parts of this book.

Standard I addresses the collection of information and three types of activities related to individual needs. Collection of information is the first step in activity programming. Criterion number one is an extensive list of the diverse information associated with an individual's activity pursuits. The other criteria address who collects the information, where it can be found, the format for collection, and the accessibility of the data. Implementing a plan of care begins with a wide-ranging collection of activity pursuit information.

The three activity categories—supportive, maintenance, and empowerment—were introduced in Chapter Two. They are defined in the standards according to individual preferences and needs, rather than types of activity media such as gardening, exercise, and games. Therapeutic value is not found in a specific activity, but in a person's positive responses. For example, listening to rock music is a fun and exhilarating activity for some, but others may find it irritating and repulsive. A facility that offers rock music programs, but has no residents who benefit from this activity, is not fulfilling the standards for activity programming. Identifying individual benefits from specific activity experiences, rather than simply providing a variety of activities, is the point from which all programming decisions are made.

Standard 2 emphasizes the importance of understanding an individual's needs and strengths. The collection of data under Standard 1 lists specific present, past, and future interests and lifestyles to explore. Comparing attitudes, abilities, and responses to past and present patterns gives the necessary information to analyze abilities and limitations.

Once an examination of an individual's strengths and needs has been completed, the activity care plan is developed as shown in Standard 3. This standard highlights the significance of involving the resident in the care plan and specifically in goal setting. Any individual who is involved in setting goal's that affect his/her life is more likely to attain a sense of autonomy. Incorporating these goals into the interdisciplinary care plan links resident activity choices with the services of other disciplines. Setting measurable goals facilitates a well-defined plan for the resident to accomplish.

Standard 4 illustrates the progression from collection of information, to analysis, to care planning, to implementation. The program to be carried out is a reflection of the collected data, analysis of strengths and needs, and the goals. Implementation is flexible regarding any temporary changes in the resident's health status. Resident involvement in this step continues to be emphasized. Safety issues are considered, and community resources are utilized.

Standard 5 starts the cycle again. Potential changes in the collected information, analysis, care planning, and implementation are reviewed. This final standard also evaluates the effectiveness of the first four standards. If a care plan has not led to positive outcomes, the collection and analysis stages are reviewed for possible lack of information, changes in information, and/or unsatisfactory analysis. The care plan is adapted according to the findings of the review. If execution of the care plan itself is found to be a problem, changes in programming, resident involvement, safety, or other aspects are revised.

Each standard is ongoing. Neither collection nor any other aspect of these standards is ever completed. As a resident's mental, physical, and psychosocial well-being deteriorates or improves, each standard is adjusted to current needs. Such adjustments require constant assessment and evolution of the relationship between the activity professional and the resident.

 **ACTIVITY THERAPY ASSESSMENT**

Many elderly who enter long-term care facilities have numerous problems impacting their physical, cognitive, emotional, and social functioning. Diagnoses can include a variety of chronic and debilitating conditions such as diabetes, cerebrovascular accidents, rheumatoid arthritis, Alzheimer's disease, and chronic obstructive pulmonary disease. Individual residents often have multiple diagnoses, making assessment difficult since it is hard to determine which symptom relates to which diagnosis. In addition, changes in perceptual acuity, bodily functions, and the nervous system happen as a normal process of aging.

The result of these deficits is an impaired ability to independently function. Many of the elderly entering long-term care have given up their homes and many of their personal possessions as well as having lost close contact with friends, spouses, and family members due to death, illness, or relocation. For many institutionalized elderly, this accumulation of losses leads to a decline in self-worth. Activity therapy assessments establish a foundation for assisting residents in regaining a sense of well-being. The activity professional will find assessment to be a dynamic, stimulating process.

Knowledge about normal aging and common diseases is imperative to making assessment judgments. This knowledge is part of curriculums for activity professional courses, but it also requires ongoing study as information on aging is continually modified. This book assumes the reader has a working knowledge of common resident functioning problems and the aging process.

In addition, each facility may have residents who are not elderly or who have atypical problems or needs. Location and type of services offered affect the common characteristics of the residents. Some facilities may specialize in services such as short-term rehabilitation, respite care, adult day care, head injuries, or Alzheimer's units. This requires the activity professional to have a general understanding of the needs of each type of resident population, e.g., head injury residents are likely to be younger than most nursing home residents and have different interests.

Determining Activity Outcomes of Care

The assessment provides a baseline for determining the activity programming services needed for residents to restore their preferred activity pursuit patterns. Assessments reveal the strengths and weaknesses of each individual in order to achieve the best results. Therapeutic goals and approaches are based on a resident's functioning, characteristics, current and past patterns, and activity preferences. Resident abilities and activity interests are key factors in addressing resident deficits and improving quality of life.

Assessment data have implications for resident outcomes and the related areas of quality assurance, regulatory surveys, residents' rights, and reimbursement. Quality assurance programs act as an evaluation tool for services provided to residents and the effects of those services. Ascertaining whether services are appropriate and outcomes are satisfactory can only be done by comparing results achieved with resident assessments.

Examining outcomes of care in long-term care facilities is a mandated part of federal surveys. Assessments are frequently used as a basis for making judgments about the quality of the services provided and whether the results are appropriate to the resident's condition. For example, if a resident is withdrawn upon admission, this condition indicates that an activity approach should be implemented to help alleviate this problem. If the activity assessment identifies the resident as an avid gardener, he/she is encouraged to participate in gardening projects. This activity could decrease the withdrawal symptoms by engaging the resident in a former activity pursuit. If the activity assessment and care plan do not adequately identify resident interests and the resident remains withdrawn, this behavior is an indicator that the facility has not provided optimal services. Surveyors are mandated to look for comprehensive assessments and the implementation of individualized approaches to determine whether resident outcomes are expected (Department of Health and Human Services, 1992).

Assessments need to identify residents' preferences to assure that residents' rights are recognized and respected by the activity staff. Documenting residents' activity choices and providing services reflecting these preferences demonstrates how assessments can lead to fulfillment of residents' rights. Many examples can be found on the sample assessment form (Figure 6.1a-e). Review Part 2 of the form where a space is provided for indicating whether a resident needs mail read and if so, indicates the individual(s) whom the resident wants to perform this task. This preference relates to the right to receive mail unopened. Even though activity personnel or volunteers are often responsible for delivering the mail and assisting residents as needed, some residents may prefer that family members or others read their mail to them. There has been an increased emphasis in recent years on residents' rights, and assessments supply evidence that these rights are being recognized.

Many states as well as the federal government are using and/or are researching the use of case mix reimbursement systems. In brief, such a system means that financial reimbursement for a resident's care is based on the type and amount of care provided to each individual, rather than a set fee regardless of needs. These systems are generally based on assessment information, and some systems are attempting to tie services provided to resident outcomes. It is important that activity assessments accurately reflect the services a resident needs and the results. For example, in many facilities, activity professionals provide the majority of transportation to and from activities. This is an important individualized service since many residents are unable to get to activities independently due to cognitive, physical, or other functioning deficits. The activity assessment should reflect the need for this service if it is provided by the activity staff. Progress notes record whether the service has been provided and the results, i.e., resident attended activities of his/her choice.

Chapter 4 discussed the vast amount of information the RAI offers to a resident assessment. This chapter will illustrate the crucial role activity assessments play in cultivating positive results by integrating the RAI data into a comprehensive activity assessment tool. This tool will also reference the practice standards described in the previous chapter. Assessment is the constant and most critical factor in programming for positive outcomes.

Collecting Information

The assessment process begins by collecting information about each resident's past and present with regard to emotional, social, cognitive, and physical functioning. Information about past, current, and future interests and lifestyle is an indicator of functional problems and the impact these problems are having on a resident. A basis for comparison is provided by including data from the past and present. Necessary sources for obtaining comprehensive information include medical charts, observation, and resident, family, and staff interviews. A review of the resident's record focuses on medical and social histories, other disciplines' assessments and the Minimum Data Set. As discussed in Chapters 3 and 4, consulting multiple sources for information leads to a more complete view of each resident.

The Activity Assessment Form

Overview

The activity assessment form provides a consistent tool for collecting the necessary data. The form is based on standards of practice and facilitates resident interviews. The assessment's design considers the type of care a facility provides, common resident characteristics, and individual activity programs. Particular items of the RAI are incorporated on the activity assessment tool to assure consistency and integration of critical information.

The sample activity assessment form should be reviewed by the reader. It would be helpful to make a copy of all the parts and use it as a reference throughout this book. On first reading, note that the form is divided into five major areas: Resident Profile (Part 1), Activity Pursuits and Related Abilities (Part 2), Support Systems (Part 3), Psychosocial and Cognitive Functioning (Part 4), and Primary Strengths and Weaknesses (Part 5). These topics illustrate the general categories an activity assessment should contain. The reader may want to compare the form's contents with Standard 1 of the Standards of Practice in Appendix C.

Since the assessment process involves an interview with the resident and/or significant others, the form's design allows for a logical, easy to follow step by step gathering of information. The sample form (Figure 6.1a-e) is arranged in a manner that helps the activity professional to ask questions, to

make observations, to gather MDS screens, and to complete the form simultaneously. In other words, this form serves as a time saving device.

The activity assessment form is adapted to each facility with regard to the type of care the setting provides, common characteristics of the residents, and the individual activity program. In a facility where many residents return home or to another level of care, the reason for placement and the goal of placement (Part 1, Figure 6.1a) are particularly important in determining the length of stay and the most realistic approaches. Part 2 of the sample form reflects one facility's specific activities based on the common interests of its residents. If the facility is located in a community where most elderly women quilt, then "quilting" may be an appropriate category to include on the form. Since every resident's interests are unique, it is important to leave adequate space to document other individual preferences. As changes occur in the setting and its population, the form is updated accordingly.

The use of dots in front of some of the items on the form indicate a relationship to specific sections of the MDS. The dots in front of the items in Part 2 relate to MDS Section I. The dots in Part 3 are tied to MDS Sections III, G, and I. This is a convenient method for integrating the MDS with the activity assessment form. Note also the form's use of "C" and "P" on Parts 2 and 3 to indicate time frames. "C" refers to the last seven days and "P" indicates from young adulthood to admission. "C" is related to the time frame most often used in completing the MDS and thus provides a link to the RAI. "P" indicates a lifetime of interests which is critical to a more comprehensive assessment of activity pursuit patterns

On second reading, the specific information about the case example, Jane Smith, (fictitious name) should be noted. This example shows how the form's structure facilitates the collection of data. Ms. Smith's case

Figure 6.1a
Activity Therapy Assessment
Part I

NAME _(fictitious name)_ Jane Smith   PREFERS Jane   RM# 101   ID# xyz   ADMIT DATE 10/5/92

RESIDENT PROFILE

Date of Birth 4/10/15   Place of Birth Atlanta, Georgia

Diagnoses Left CVA, Aphasia

Reason for Placement Dependence in ADLs   Goal Lower Level of Care

Mode of Transportation to Activities Wheelchair with total assistance

Precautions / Allergies Relevant to the AT Care Plan None noted

AT Endurance Level I

Diet Regular

PT Discontinued in hospital   OT Discontinued in hospital   ST Discontinued in hospital

was introduced in Chapter 4, page 23. The reader should review the narrative summary in Chapter 4 and note how this information is documented within the form's structure. This case will be referred to throughout the rest of this book. When Ms. Smith's assessment is not useful to a specific explanation, other resident cases will be presented.

Some activity professionals use a narrative assessment rather than a specific form. The author recommends a form since it is easy to spot specific areas, e.g., interests and religious affiliation which can be relevant to approaches. In addition, a form provides a consistent baseline for identifying individual outcomes and trends in program results. If a narrative assessment is used, it is important to follow a standardized outline. This outline could include many of the items listed on the sample form. Regardless of the specific assessment method, the amount of individualized information gathered is the validating factor.

Completing the Assessment Form

Most of the information for Part 1—Resident Profile (Figure 6.1a) is obtained from the medical chart. The activity professional then begins the resident interview at Part 2—Activity Pursuits and Related Abilities (Figure 6.1b). This interview starts with items the resident will probably find easy to discuss, i.e., occupation, education, and interests. When activity preferences are explored, it is important to remember that past interests include young adulthood up to admission to the facility. Residents who suffer from many functioning problems often have few current or future interests based on the belief that they no longer have the necessary abilities to pursue activities. An expansive activity pursuit history broadens the options and adaptations that can be offered.

Once interests are recorded, the activity professional explains the activity services available, incorporating the information just learned about the resident's preferences. The resident is asked which programs or individual services he/she would like to participate in during a specified time period. If the

**Figure 6.1b
Activity Therapy Assessment
Part 2**

ACTIVITY PURSUITS & RELATED ABILITIES

(C) - *Indicates Current Over Last Seven Days* **(P)** - *Indicates Young Adulthood to Admission*

Occupation(s): Homemaker, School Teacher & Professional Singer

Education: Bachelor's Degree in Education

School(s) Attended: Atlanta Grade & High Schools, University of Georgia

Politics: **(P & C)** Active in the Democratic Party   **Desire to Vote** Yes

- **Cards/Other Games:** **(P)** Played cards with friends, gin rummy was favorite card game
- **Crafts/Arts:** **(P)** Water color painting, participated in alone & for recreation
- **Exercise/Sports:** **(P or C)** No interest
- **Music:** **(P & C)** Sang professionally for churches & community concerts, enjoys listening to & performing gospel and jazz
- **Reading:** **(P)** Reading the bible and history, but now is unable to read due to visual deficits; indicated no interest in book tape service
- **Writing:** **(P)** Used to write letters to family and friends.

Eyesight: Right visual field cut   **Small Print ( ) or Large Print ( ) is desirable**

Needs Mail Read (x) If yes, resident gives permission for Activity Staff **to read mail.**

- **Trips/Shopping:** **(P)** Travelled across the country; enjoyed clothes shopping
- **Walking/Wheeling Outdoors:** **(P)** No desire to go outside at this time
- **Watching TV:** **(P & C)** Watches soap operas on Channel 4 in the afternoon

Intergenerational Activities Desired: **(P&C)** Enjoys grandchildren & enjoyed teaching children

Pets: Does not like pets of any kind

Gardening: **(P)** Spent several hours a week caring for house plants, indicates no interest now

Cooking: **(P)** Took pleasure in cooking for family, especially baking pies

Other Life Involvements: None known at this time.

Use of Hands: (Right) No muscular control   **(Left)** Good fine & gross motor

- **Preferred Activity Settings (x) Own Rm   ( ) Day/Activity Rm   ( ) Inside/Off Unit   ( ) Outside Facility   ( ) None**

Group & Individual Activities Resident States He/She Will Participate In No group preferences. Enjoys listening to radio when gospel music is played. Expressed discomfort about activities outside her room

- **More or Different Activity Preferences/Choices Not Currently Offered:** Resident expresses no other choices, but frequently refuses invitations to group activities that reflect P & C interests.

Resident's Perception of Current Abilities/Interests: Indicated a lack of interest in many past involvements, apparently due to decline in physical status, e.g., decreased eyesight & use of right side. She pointed to her right hand when asked about past interests, e.g., gardening.

- **Significance of Resident's Time Awake & Time Spent In Activities:** Resident's limited activity involvement increases her feelings of isolation as evidenced by frequent calling out to staff for items she can reach

> • (dot) relates to MDS Items

assessment is part of a routine annual evaluation, the time interval refers to the next three months or until the next care plan review. For new admissions or residents who are experiencing a significant change in their condition, a more propitious time period is one month or less. For these residents, it is important to track progress frequently until they become familiar with the facility and/or their condition stabilizes. At the review interval, the activity professional assesses whether the resident is establishing the activity pursuit pattern of his/her choice.

Examining the desire to participate furnishes clues about perceptions of abilities and information about how a resident is adjusting to facility placement. Part 2 of the assessment form lists More or Different Activity Preferences/Choices Not Currently Offered and Resident's Perception of Current Abilities/Interests as further probes into a resident's potential for meaningful involvement in activities. When the activity professional asks these questions, they provide important care planning information while engaging the resident in a more in-depth conversation about activity choices. In the case of Ms. Jane Smith, she indicates many past interests, but shows little desire to participate in current activities. It is possible she is not adjusting to the facility and/or she is uncertain if she has the ability to engage in activity preferences. This lack of interest may also suggest that none of the activity group or individual services match her interests well enough to promote participation.

Once activity pursuits are explored, the interview leads to Part 3—Support Systems (Figure 6.1c). Here, the resident is asked questions primarily about relationships. Some of this information is obtained from the social service history. Since positive participation in group activities is dependent on the ability to socialize with others, it is valuable for the activity professional to collect data about a resident's current and past relationships.

Support from people outside the facility provides a familiar link to the present unfamiliar situation. The items listed under Support Systems give specific ideas for care plan approaches. For example, Ms. Jane Smith's children and church members visit weekly. Though Ms. Smith's history indicates she was quite active in her church and volunteered in her community, she does not wish to become involved in the facility's religious or community service programs. Ms. Smith's children or church friends are valuable resources for engaging her in these activities. A close friend from the church could be asked to contact the minister to provide services at the facility. The friend also could join Ms. Smith in one of the facility's community service programs.

Much of the data for Part 4—Psychosocial & Cognitive Functioning (Figure 6.1d) are based on responses made throughout the interview. Deficits and strengths in orientation, communication, hearing, mood, and behavior usually become evident from answers to questions from the previous sections. Waiting until the end of the interview to complete this part allows time for multiple observations of resident skills.

Part 5—Primary Strengths and Weaknesses (Figure 6.1e) is a summary of the assessment. No new information is introduced here. This recap is the basis for writing the activity care plan.

The resident should be encouraged to describe his/her strengths and weaknesses during the interview as an initial step toward participation in the care plan. For example, after interviewing Ms. Smith about her interests and support systems, the activity professional, Karen Frost, ACC, asks her what she feels are her primary strengths. Due to Ms. Smith's limited communication skills, Ms. Frost asks yes/no questions. Ms. Smith replies "Yes" when asked if she considers her singing ability and her family as strengths. Refer to Part 5 of the form where these are listed as "Current Ability and Interest in

Figure 6.1c
Activity Therapy Assessment
Part 3

SUPPORT SYSTEMS

(C) - Indicates Current Over Last Seven Days   *(P)- Indicates Young Adulthood to Admission*

Marital Status _____W_____ **Name of Spouse** Alfred Smith

Relationship with Spouse ____ (P & C) According to her daughter, Millie Hamlin, she had a close relationship with her husband, & "She adjusted well when he died."

Relationship with Children ____ (P & C) Resident smiled and stated "Yes, ma'am" when her family was mentioned. Family members appear to be supportive, visiting one time weekly. Resident has 3 sons and 1 daughter.

• **Spiritual/Religious Activities** ____ (P & C) Temple Baptist in Monarch, Georgia

• **Involvement Patterns** ____ (P & C) Active involvement throughout her adult life, teaching Sunday School and singing in the choir. Church members & minister visit weekly.

Organizational Memberships & Community Involvement ____ (P & C) Served on committees for the Women's Social Club of Monarch; members do not visit resident or involve her in activities at this time. Community concert choir director, Margaret Goforth, visits occasionally.

Other Support Systems ____ (P & C) Neighbors visit occasionally. She has formed a close relationship with one nursing assistant, Deanna. Resident & Deanna often sing together during resident's morning care.

Living Arrangement Prior to Facility Placement ____ Lived independently prior to recent hospitalization

• **Identification with Past Roles & Lifestyle** ____ Resident became animated when asked about past activity pursuits & support systems.

> **• (dot) relates to MDS items**

Singing" and "Supportive Family and Community." Family members also assist in identifying strengths. Ms. Smith's daughter says, "Mother is very fond of her nursing assistant, Deanna, and she has always had many interests." These are listed as "Relationship with Nursing Assistant" and "Past Interest in Many Activity Pursuits." The same strategy is used with Weaknesses.

Information about sensitivity to items such as flowers or specific foods, alcohol tolerance, or behaviors such as removing restraints are important factors to record. As with all items, the information obtained depends on each individual activity program. Precautions/allergies relevant to the Activity Therapy (AT) care plan, diet, and AT endurance level are included on the form under Part 1—Resident Profile. Observations regarding specific moods and behavior can be found under Part 4. The activity professional keeps an easily accessible master list of any pertinent data related to each resident's diet, endurance level, or unsafe behaviors for quick referral. For example, when an activity involves serving food, the list is checked to identify individuals with special diets or those who are prone to choking. Other activity staff and/or volunteers need access to this list to assure awareness of any special precautions for residents.

Figure 6.1d
Activity Therapy Assessment
Part 4

PSYCHOSOCIAL & COGNITIVE FUNCTIONING

Orientation Unable to state situation, time, place or person, but facial expressions, yes/no response & gestures indicate she is oriented x 4.

Memory: Recent Good, remembers family's visits.

   Remote Good, able to indicate past interests accurately.

Communication Able to answer yes/no questions accurately, makes understandable gestures for basic needs, i.e., drink, bathroom. Facial expressions indicate moods & feelings. Uses singing as a form of expression.

Hearing Understands questions when a normal speaking voice is used.

Response to Interview(s) Friendly, smiling and laughing, but became frustrated when she was unable to make her answers clear.

Observations Regarding Specific Mood & Behavior Refused to hold her cup of water for a drink & wanted interviewer to hold it for her though she is able to do this herself.

Figure 6.1e
Activity Therapy Assessment
Part 5

PRIMARY STRENGTHS & WEAKNESSES

Strengths Past Interest in Many Activity Pursuits

Current Ability & Interest in Singing

Supportive Family & Community

Relationship with Nursing Assistant

Oriented

Good Left Hand Fine & Gross Motor Skills

Weaknesses Feels Unloved/Needs Attention

Decreased Mobility

Poor Communication Skills

Limited Current Involvement in
Activity Pursuits

Other Comments: Nursing staff report that she demands attention frequently by turning her call light on, with no specific request. She refuses to propel her wheelchair though she has the ability to be independent in wheelchair mobility. Some of lifestyle & support system information was provided by resident's daughter, Millie Hamlin. Ms. Hamlin stated the family's relationship with resident has "always been very close."

SIGNATURE   *Karen Frost, ACC*   **DATE**   10/19/92

Identifying the Assessment Form's Relation to the RAI

The MDS is the initial step to activity assessments. Particular MDS items can be linked to activity assessment forms to assure consistency, integration of information and follow up. The activity professional also coordinates the RAP renew process with the completion of the activity assessment. When the RAI is integrated into daily practice through activity assessments, a powerful system for achieving resident outcomes is put into motion

The MDS and the activity therapy assessment evaluate similar areas while serving different functions. Before proceeding, the reader is encouraged to look over the items of the MDS (Appendix A) and consider their relevance to activity assessment. The MDS acts as a screening tool that draws attention to overall functioning, characteristics, and patterns by asking general, standardized questions. Strict coding procedures are followed to obtain results. The activity therapy assessment provides a detailed picture of resident functioning, characteristics, and patterns in relation to activity pursuit patterns. This assessment is based on professional practice standards. Completion incorporates specific resident comments and responses with assessor observations. It uses descriptive statements rather than specific coding criteria. The MDS focuses primarily on the last seven days while the activity therapy assessment views the individual's entire life history.

Cross referencing the MDS and the activity therapy assessment integrates information and saves time. Placing some of the MDS screening items on the activity therapy assessment form helps gather general and specific information concurrently, thus reducing duplicative efforts.

As noted previously, the sample activity assessment form (Figure 6.1a-e) contains items from several sections of the MDS. These MDS items (indicated with a dot) include Section III Customary Routines, Section G-Psychosocial Well-Being, and Section I-Activity Pursuit Patterns. Wording sometimes varies slightly, but the intent is the same.

All five items from MDS Section I are included in Figure 4.1, Activity Pursuit Patterns (page 20). MDS Section I-Item 1 Time Awake and Item 2 Average Time Involved In Activities are combined in the last item under Part 2 of the activity assessment form (Figure 6.1b). The activity professional can provide a summary of how the resident's time awake and activity involvement positively or negatively affect quality of life.

MDS Section I—Item 3 Preferred Activity Settings is located toward the end of Part 2 of the assessment form (Figure 6.1b). Here, the activity assessment has only a space for check marks; however, the item "Group and Individual Activities Resident States He/She Will Participate In" is a place to expand if needed. This is done with Ms. Smith who includes only her room as an activity setting preference.

The assessment form is designed to enhance the flow of an interview therefore the items from MDS Section I sometimes appear in a different order. Compare MDS Section I—Item 4 General Activity Preferences (Appendix A-4, page 121) to the activity preferences in Parts 2 and 3 of the assessment form (Figure 6.1b and c). Note the differences in succession, e.g., "spiritual/religious" activities is listed in Part 3 since it is pertinent to support systems.

MDS Section I—Item 5 Prefers More or Different Activities is listed toward the bottom of Part 2 (Figure 6.1b). As indicated on Ms. Smith's assessment, the assessment form records more details about her activity choices. It shows that she has been offered activities reflecting her past and current interests, but she declines involvement if the activities take place outside her room. Offering one-on-one opportunities in her room where she is more receptive is suggested from these observations.

A potential time saving device is to complete the MDS related items on the activity assessment form before coding MDS Section I. For example, the activity professional, Ms. Frost, completes those questions proceeded with dots on the assessment form (Figure 6.1b and c) before completing the MDS Section I. She uses the "C" abbreviation to indicate current interests over the last seven days. She now has the necessary data to accurately code MDS Section I without spending additional time.

Coding the MDS gives a minute perspective on a given item while the activity assessment identifies an expansive record of a resident's activity pursuit pattern. The information collected on Ms. Smith's activity assessment form is more detailed than the coding on the MDS. Refer to the sample activity assessment form under crafts/arts (Figure 6.1b). The information about the specific type of art Ms. Smith has enjoyed and her past pattern of participating in this art alone and for recreation (as opposed to work) provide important clues for developing individualized approaches. The value of specific information about resident preferences is discussed in detail later in this chapter.

Parts of the MDS Customary Routine Section III and the MDS Psychosocial Well-Being Section G (Appendix A) are integrated with the activity assessment form. Compare activity assessment items "Involvement Patterns" and "Identification with Past Roles & Lifestyle" in Part 3 (Figure 6.1c) with these two MDS sections. Ms. Smith's assessment illustrates how details about these areas can provide substance for planning.

Once the MDS trigger conditions are identified, the RAP review process begins. If one or more of the Activities Triggers are present, the activity professional reviews the Activities RAP (Appendix B) while filling out the assessment form. Completing the form leads to answers raised by the RAPs and the RAPs may stimulate questions that are not already covered by the form. For example, Ms. Smith's assessment indicates a lack of interest in activity pursuits (review Part 2, Figure 6.1b of the activity assessment form under "Resident's Perception of Current Abilities/Interests"). Compare the information in this section to the Activities RAP Guideline (Appendix B) question "Recent decline in resident status". The "guidelines" offer additional insight into Ms. Smith's lack of activity involvement.

The activity professional is also aware of related Activities Triggers and RAPs. For example, the activity assessment provides information about psychosocial functioning. If a resident "triggers" in the areas of psychosocial well-being, mood state or behavior problems, the activity professional will compare these particular RAPs with the activity assessment. Any findings are shared with the individual(s) (if other than the activity professional) who is completing these RAPs.

The MDS, the RAPs, and the activity assessment serve vital evaluation functions. While the MDS is a standardized tool, it does not provide the specificity of information needed to develop individualized approaches. The RAPs provide additional assessment questions around specific problem areas. Integrating particular MDS items onto the activity assessment form and then completing the RAP review process and the activity assessment, simultaneously links the RAI to the comprehensive care plan.

Studying Patterns

The activity assessment includes an examination of lifelong activity pursuit patterns and lifestyle choices. Studying patterns is especially important to the activity assessment since it reveals a broader picture of the resident's potential. This involves a review of lifestyle from early adulthood to the present, noting when changes occurred and evaluating circumstances surrounding the changes.

A method of documentation is necessary for tracking these patterns. As mentioned previously, the assessment form (Figure 6.1b and c) uses the letter "P" to indicate past and the letter "C" to indicate current patterns. These abbreviations are a convenient method for studying patterns.

Learning when changes in lifestyle happened helps to identify the focus of activity interventions and how long it will take before a positive outcome will occur. The timing of a pattern alteration may be related to illness, social losses, financial difficulties, mental illness, or other stressful situations. Connecting a change to the circumstances surrounding it provides a wealth of information about why the change occurred and what factors are related to it.

Length of illness as mentioned in Chapter 3 under *Determining Outcomes* is one consideration in determining when changes in lifestyle began to take place and what strategy is most likely to be effective. Short periods of illness usually mean that a *continuation* of recent lifestyle patterns will occur rapidly. Approaches center on maintaining this pattern during the acute illness and after discharge. A lengthy illness usually requires *restoration* of past lifestyle routines and takes a longer period of time for recovery. Approaches concentrate on a gradual recuperation of a familiar lifestyle pattern.

For example, a female resident recently moved to the area and is admitted to a facility with a fractured hip. Prior to her move, she lived independently and was quite active, walking for long distances, driving, housekeeping, socializing with friends, and pursuing hobbies. She is lethargic due to the severity of her acute condition. The activity approaches primarily support her in *continuing* her recent lifestyle pattern. Since she just moved to the area, the approaches

involve educating her about the community's resources and helping her make social contacts. It is expected that this resident will quickly begin participating in activity pursuits and socializing with new friends. Barring complications, she will return to independent living and essentially the same lifestyle.

Another female resident is admitted with a fractured hip. She moved to the area a year ago but rarely exercised and did not make friends or become involved in the community. Her lethargy is due to her acute condition as well as a lack of physical exercise, lengthy social isolation, and minimal recent participation in hobbies. The recovery period is likely to be extensive. The initial approaches *restore* her interest in an active lifestyle. The first approach is to develop a relationship with her and to begin to renew her regard for activity pursuits by providing information and individual activity opportunities in her room. A resident who has developed a pattern of social isolation may not choose attendance in group activities for several months.

Studying lifelong preferences, when changes occurred, and the circumstances surrounding them begins at admission. These patterns continually evolve and must be tracked routinely. When changes are noted during a resident's stay, several steps are taken to determine why. These steps include interviewing the resident, reviewing activity participation records, and consulting other team members. A pattern variation may or may not require an intervention. A resident may develop a new relationship and decrease activity involvement in other areas. This probably does not merit a change in the care plan. Another resident may have suffered an acute illness. The intervention may include gradually rebuilding the resident's involvement pattern to its previous level. Ongoing assessments track changes and act as a preventive measure by catching problems or needs before they become significant.

Assessment of Physical, Emotional, Social, and Cognitive Functioning

Activity assessments concentrate on a resident's functioning as it affects participation in activity pursuits. The items related to functioning on the assessment form are intended to record data that impacts activity involvement. A resident who receives physical, occupational, and/or speech therapy services frequently has less time and energy available for activity pursuits. Having this information assists the activity professional in adapting activities to meet the resident's scheduling needs and physical limitations. This section of the text will provide examples of how to evaluate the influence functioning has on activity pursuit patterns.

The MDS will be used as a reference point for identifying general resident functioning. It can be a helpful tool in completing the activity therapy assessment, but, as previously established, more activity-related information is usually needed to supplement these areas. For example, while the MDS provides information about a resident's ability to move a wheelchair independently (Section E—Physical Functioning, and Structural Problems—Item 5) and about a resident's cognitive abilities (Section B—Cognitive Patterns), it does not identify what type of help a resident needs to get to a group activity.

Physical Assessment

Diagnoses

Assessment of a resident's physical status is done by collecting information about diagnoses, physical endurance, mobility level, eyesight, hearing, communication skills, and manual dexterity. A review of the medical history and the MDS will show the primary physical diagnoses. This review furnishes a framework for problem identification in current functioning. For example, if a resident has a diagnosis of left cerebral vascular accident, special attention is paid in assessing the functional use of the resident's right side. If a resident has a diagnosis of Alzheimer's disease, the severity of disorientation as well as preserved strengths are the focus for observation.

PHYSICAL ASSESSMENTS

COLLECT INFORMATION ON:

- **Diagnoses**
- **Physical Endurance**
- **Mobility Level**
- **Eyesight**
- **Hearing**
- **Communication Skills**
- **Manual Dexterity**

Physical Endurance

Providing safe therapeutic activities that do not conflict with the physician's treatment plan requires that each resident's endurance for physical activity is accurately identified. In the past, physician's orders for activity programs have been a frequently neglected area. "Activities as tolerated" has been a common doctor's order even though it is not a clear guideline and leaves the decision of appropriate physical endurance to the activity professional rather than the physician. The resident's physician is clearly the appropriate professional to decide a resident's physical capabilities and the point at which physical activity may be harmful.

The activity therapy endurance level form shown in Figure 6.2 was developed according to the activities offered in a specific facility. An analysis of the activities identified the most strenuous activities to the least strenuous. The activities then were grouped into levels that best showed the amount of endurance required if the resident participated fully. Each resident's physician gave an order for the appropriate level (I, II, III, or IV). Using a specific order gives the activity professional a clear direction regarding each resident's physical capabilities.

Establishing this type of endurance level requires the activity professional to educate the medical staff within the facility as well as the physicians who admit residents. Training of nursing staff, especially the staff who takes doctors' orders, is crucial to successful implementation of an appropriate level. Staff in-services related to specific types of activities and the levels are helpful. Physicians also need to be informed about the types of activities in the facility, the physical endurance involved and the reasons for obtaining a specific order, i.e., safety.

In one facility where the author used this format, it became a public relation's tool. Though there was some initial implementation resistance due to the change in format, the physicians' awareness of the activity program increased dramatically for two reasons. Every time the physician admitted a resident, he/she had to decide what level of activities in which the resident could participate safely. Additionally, when the physician recommended a resident not participate in certain activities, the resident asked the doctor for an explanation.

The author believes that physicians' orders for out-of-facility trips and alcoholic beverages should be reviewed periodically. Since each out-of-facility trip may involve a different level of physical endurance, the activity professional needs to carefully consider what would be the most practical and safest procedure. A resident whose physical status varies dramatically from week to week may need an order each time he/she takes a trip out of the facility; this would assure the order matches the particular trip to this resident's abilities at a specific point in time. However, this order may not be necessary for some residents who have a relatively stable physical status and in situations where the trips involve essentially the same type of physical endurance. Some facilities have an order signed by the physician upon admission that states the recommendations regarding trips outside the facility. The author's concern about such orders is that they are not always updated when changes occur in the resident's status.

Orders for alcoholic beverages present similar concerns. The activity professional needs to develop an order that assures attention is given to alcohol's interaction with any current medications. The most conservative approach is to obtain an order every time alcohol is served; however, this procedure may also restrict a resident's freedom due to the amount of time involved in obtaining these orders. Good communication between the nursing staff and the activity professional will help ensure that orders are safe and reasonable.

Regardless of the endurance level, out-of-facility trip recommendations, or orders for alcoholic beverages, residents' rights play a role in the actual choice made. Residents need education regarding safe activity participation so they can make informed choices about their preferences. This sometimes means negotiating with residents to discover a safe level while assuring their autonomy.

Mobility Level

The term "mobility," as it is used here, refers to transfer skills, ambulation, and/or wheelchair mobility. Pertinent information about each resident's level of mobility is found on nursing, physical therapy, and occupational therapy assessments as well as the MDS. The activity professional also needs to observe each individual's mobility skills. The specificity of the information gathered is directly dependent on how it will be used. If the activity staff does not assist with ambulation and transfers, the only

Figure 6.2
Activity Therapy Endurance Level

NAME ___Jane Smith___ ROOM # ___101___ ID # ___xyz___

[X] **LEVEL I—MAXIMALLY ACTIVE**

The physician recommends that the resident can safely participate in sitting position activities involving any of the following:

    A. LIGHT AEROBIC SPORTS INCORPORATING MILD RESISTIVE EXERCISE
       Examples: Adaptive Volley Ball, Adaptive Shuffleboard, & Wheelchair Races

    B. ACTIVE, APPROPRIATE RANGE OF MOTION EXERCISES
       Examples: Exercise Classes, Adaptive Gardening

    C. LIGHT MANUAL, FINE MOTOR EXERCISES
       Examples: Writing, Operating a Tape Recorder

    D. PASSIVE LISTENING

[ ] **LEVEL II—MODERATELY ACTIVE (DELETE A)**

The physician recommends that the resident can safely participate in sitting position activities involving any of the following:

    B. ACTIVE, APPROPRIATE RANGE OF MOTION EXERCISES

    C. LIGHT MANUAL, FINE MOTOR EXERCISES

    D. PASSIVE LISTENING

[ ] **LEVEL III—MILDLY ACTIVE (DELETE A & B)**

The physician recommends that the resident can safely participate in sitting position activities involving any of the following:

    C. LIGHT MANUAL, FINE MOTOR EXERCISES

    D. PASSIVE LISTENING

[ ] **LEVEL IV—MINIMALLY ACTIVE (DELETE A, B, & C)**

    D. PASSIVE LISTENING

SIGNATURE ___Karen Frost, ACC___ DATE ___10/5/92___

information needed about mobility may be the type of transportation required for the resident to attend activities.

Eyesight

The initial activity assessment acquires as many details about eyesight as possible. Decisions about appropriate reading material, visual aids, and special approaches, such as reading mail, are dependent on this evaluation. Vague terms like "good" or "bad" eyesight do not provide sufficient information for determining the services needed. MDS Section D—Vision Patterns has useful data.

Eyesight can be checked in a practical way by asking the resident to read aloud samples of small and large print. This is an opportunity to observe the resident's visual *and* reading abilities. If the resident can read some words clearly and distorts or leaves out others (in either size print), this may indicate perceptual problems related to a stroke or poor cognitive functioning related to a dementia. If a resident cannot read either size print, this may indicate that the resident is a candidate for taped reading material such as "Talking Books."[1] If a resident is discovered to be illiterate, the activity professional will not expect the resident to perform tasks he/she is not capable of, i.e., reading the activity calendar to determine programs of interest. A resident who had a recent stroke may have visual deficits but may not be aware that these deficits have affected his/her reading ability. Simply asking this resident if he/she can read may not provide an accurate picture.

Observations of residents in specific activities over a period of time is necessary to complete an assessment of how vision impacts activity participation. A visual deficit may be obvious during the initial evaluation, but the appropriate adaptation may evolve over time,

---

1. The Talking Books program is a tape service provided through the National Library Service for the blind and physically handicapped of the Library of Congress. Access to this service may be obtained through local libraries.

e.g., a blind resident who enjoys gardening is unable to plant seeds but learns to use sensory skills of touch to transplant. Ongoing evaluation of participation deficits and abilities uncovers adaptations necessary to successful involvement.

Hearing

Hearing can be monitored by changing the interviewer's voice volume while asking questions; the clarity of the answers gives information about how well the message was understood. Open-ended questions requiring a specific answer rather than a yes or no response are preferred. For example, "What type of music do you like?" as opposed to "Do you like music?" When a resident's responses are inconsistent despite the use of a clear loud speaking voice, severe hearing impairment and/or a deficit in cognitive functioning may be involved. Refer also to MDS Section C—Communication/Hearing Patterns for basic information about hearing. Speech Language Pathologists and Audiologists are consulted regarding appropriate hearing amplification devices and specific techniques.

Additional information is obtained during one-on-one or group participation. Some residents prefer to sit at the back of the room for certain types of music programs since the higher pitches are irritating at close range and tolerable at a distance. These same residents may prefer sitting close to the front for discussion groups. Observations related to a resident's auditory acuity leads to the development of approaches that address specific hearing impairments and situations.

Communication Skills

A resident, who is unable to communicate with lucidity or consistency, suffers from isolation and frustration unless steps are taken to accurately assess and improve communication skills and to adapt the environment to decrease barriers. Assessment of skills includes observing verbal communication, including the clarity of speech and the appropriateness of speech, and assessing nonverbal communication such as behavior and gestures. MDS Section C—Communication/Hearing Patterns and Speech/Language Pathologists are both excellent resources to consult.

Verbal communication deficits vary widely. Residents who have suffered a stroke may have slurred speech, and the content may or may not be appropriate. Residents who have a dementia may have clear speech, but the words spoken may be irrelevant to the situation. When verbal communication is impaired, nonverbal communication becomes a critical tool for comprehending a resident's needs and preferences. Facial expressions, attentiveness and eye contact are clues for understanding what a resident is communicating. When gestures, such as pointing and waving, are the primary source of communication, understanding their meaning is important in relating to the resident.

Overtime, as the resident is routinely observed, approaches are developed to maximize communication. Repeated observations in a variety of settings show the techniques and the environment best suited to resident needs. For example, the activity professional notices that a confused resident begins to wander and talk incoherently when placed in the activity room during a large group reminiscent activity. During small group reminiscent activities, the resident is able to sit and reminisce clearly about the past. An important piece of assessment information has been learned about how to improve the resident's communication, i.e., have the resident participate in a reminiscent group activity where the stimulation is limited.

For a resident with poor communication skills, it is difficult to assess preferences during the initial interview. This is especially true since the interview usually takes place in the resident's room or one location. Demonstration of activity opportunities is limited by the activity equipment available in this location and by verbal explanations which may or may not be understood. Identification

of specific interests is improved by watching a resident participate in a variety of activities. When a resident comes to the activity room where he/she can observe and participate, it is easier to communicate specific preferences. Mr. Maynard, a resident who is able to use only gestures and yes/no responses for communication, indicates during the initial assessment that he has a past interest in gardening. When asked if he will participate in gardening while in the facility, he states, "no." When the activity professional takes him to the activity room during a garden class where raised beds and other adaptive equipment are used, Mr. Maynard starts to participate. In this case, better communication occurred by using a visual experience to show the resident a specific activity opportunity. Assessment of communication skills and interests is enhanced by taking the resident to activity programs and/or providing activity demonstrations on a one-on-one basis.

Manual Dexterity

Lack of information about manual dexterity or effective adaptations leads either to inappropriate placement in an activity requiring skills the resident lacks or to the exclusion of the resident from participating in an activity that is considered no longer feasible. Manual dexterity can be tested by asking the resident to touch each finger consecutively to the thumb (fine motor skills) and then to make a tight fist (gross motor skills).

Another place to look for related information is the dietary and/or nursing assessments of the resident's feeding ability and MDS Section E—Physical Functioning and Structural Problems. If residents can feed themselves independently or with partial assistance, this indicates an *ability* with regard to manual dexterity. Adaptations then can be designed based on deficits, skills and interests. For example, a resident who enjoys handwork has poor fine motor skills but good gross motor skills. Sewing quilting stitches may be frustrating while stuffing a pillow may be readily accomplished.

Observing the resident in specific activities, trying a variety of adaptations, and consulting other professionals increases resident involvement. For example, Mr. Johnston had played the guitar for most of his life prior to a recent stroke which significantly affected the use of his left side. In consultation with the physical and occupational therapists, the activity professional discovers that Mr. Johnston is not expected to regain any use of his left hand. He expresses a continued interest in music participation. On the advice of a music therapist, the activity professional asks Mr. Johnston if he would be willing to try learning how to play an omnichord. The omnichord has buttons that are pushed using one hand. Since each chord sustains until another chord is played, Mr. Johnston is able to use the strum plate until he changes to the next chord. The activity professional coaches Mr. Johnston on how to use the omnichord, and with practice he is able to use the instrument without assistance. This gives Mr. Johnston an opportunity to participate in an activity similar to his past interest and adapted for his current abilities.

Emotional Assessment

Much of a person's emotional health emanates from a satisfying activity pursuit pattern. Lack of involvement can cause or magnify emotional problems. At the same time, activity pursuits can positively intervene in mood and behavior. Ongoing activity therapy assessment offers a critical intervention for some of the most difficult problems faced by residents in long-term care and builds a firm structure for the experience of quality of life.

Assessment of a resident's emotional status is done by reviewing the diagnoses, observing the resident's responses to the current situation, comparing current responses to past lifestyle, and analyzing key sections of the MDS. Psychiatric and medical diagnoses provide initial clues to residents' emotional symptoms. A working knowledge of how specific psychiatric and medical illnesses impact emotional functioning is necessary to the design of activity plans. A diagnosis of mental illness such as depression, manic depression, or schizophrenia requires planning that anticipates the probable impact on activity participation. For example, the interests of a resident who has a bipolar disorder may vary dramatically with the disease's cycles. The activity care plan should be designed so that these changes are foreseen and adaptations are quickly made to accommodate maximum activity involvement. Medical diagnoses such as strokes or dementia also affect mood and behavior. A resident who has suffered a stroke may have labile emotional responses, e.g., resident cries during happy or neutral events. A resident with dementia may experience catastrophic reactions in a stimulating environment.

EMOTIONAL ASSESSMENT

Review:	Diagnoses
Observe:	Response to Current Situation
Compare:	Current Responses to Past Lifestyle
Analyze:	MDS Sections

Responses to the current situation are identified by asking questions about placement in the facility, current functioning status, and lifestyle preferences. Asking these questions usually elicits emotional responses. As mentioned in the overview, residents in long-term care facilities suffer multiple losses. It is critical to assess how each resident is coping with these circumstances.

Individuals who are experiencing difficulty often respond positively to familiar activities that are readily accomplished. Familiar activities then establish a sense of confidence in the current setting and allow for the expression of feelings. For example, Ms.

Hightower describes her recent deterioration in health status and placement in the facility as "tragic" and her lifestyle as one of "dependency." She states further, "I used to be very independent, even mowed my own grass until I fell. Now, I can't do anything but sit and wait." These feelings need to receive attention before Ms. Hightower will be able to focus on involvement in the life of the facility. The activity professional and Ms. Hightower develop an activity care plan that initially includes familiar activities Ms. Hightower can easily do, i.e., music listening, visiting with family members, and caring for a plant. One morning, as Ms. Hightower is watering a plant in her room, she begins to discuss the garden she planted every year and how she misses it. The activity provides Ms. Hightower with a safe avenue for expressing feelings about the current situation. Once her losses are expressed and become less emotionally consuming, she is likely to explore new activities and to make new friendships.

Responses to the current situation are compared to past attitudes and preferences to gain a more complete, individualized perspective. Patterns that remain the same are generally an indicator that the resident is coping well with the current situation. Life patterns that have shifted with the onset of physical deterioration merit close investigation to determine if the changes have resulted in a decline of emotional health. In Ms. Hightower's example, her belief that she could no longer do anything independently reflected her internal feelings of loss.

A comparison of current interests and lifestyle to those of the past is done by examining the resident's desire to be involved in the activity program. If a resident was once highly involved in numerous activity pursuits but now refuses to participate in similar activities in the long-term care facility, this current response is an altered behavior pattern. If this response is a recent change, it is probably related to the resident's adjustment to recent events. If it has occurred over a long period of time, it may be related to

a progressive decline in some or all aspects of functioning. A resident who has a lifetime routine of preferring sedentary and solitary activities and now expresses the same preferences is indicating a desire to continue a similar behavior pattern. For this individual, an activity pattern of low physical effort and limited socialization reflects a desire for a continued lifestyle rather than an indication of emotional maladjustment.

The MDS Sections G—Psychosocial Well-Being, H—Mood and Behavior Patterns, and I—Activity Pursuit Patterns (Appendix A) encompass emotional functioning data. The relevance of Section I to emotional functioning was discussed in Chapter 4. Section G examines a sense of initiative, unsettled relationships, and identification with past roles. Since most of the MDS items refer to the past seven days, past and present comparisons are especially pertinent to designing realistic goals and approaches. For example, Mr. Snodgrass' MDS Section G indicates that he "openly expresses conflict/anger with family or friends." In checking with the social worker, the activity professional finds that Mr. Snodgrass has never had a positive relationship with his family. While this area still needs to be addressed, the specific approaches and goals are dependent on both the current and past emotional pattern, i.e., a realistic goal may be to reduce the conflict rather than eliminate it.

A key area to review in MDS Section G is under Part 3—Past Roles. Most people identify strongly with their past life status. If this area is not checked, it would deserve further exploration. A resident's lack of strong identification (Item 3a) may denote a sense of feeling useless. Specific activity programs, such as oral history or reminiscence groups, are effective interventions. Expression of sadness over lost roles (Item 3b) can be positively addressed by offering the resident an important function in the facility such as volunteering as a friendly visitor or mail carrier. One-to-one listening or support groups also assist the grieving process.

Section H—Mood and Behavior Patterns records additional components of emotional functioning. One aspect of mood and behavior that is important to explore is when patterns emerge. Do, for example, aggressive behaviors occur during ADL care, during specific activities, or during family visits? This yields insight into why these responses happen and how to decrease or eliminate them.

Activity care plans are a viable method for intervening in negative mood and behavior problems. Sports activities offer an outlet for aggressive behavior. Small group or one-on-one activities provide a less stimulating and/or more comfortable atmosphere for agitated or fearful residents. Residents who resist care are more cooperative when they have a favorite activity to get dressed for and/or their favorite music is played during ADL care.

Section H also identifies potential safety concerns. Symptoms, such as motor agitation, wandering, verbal abuse, and physical abuse, merit special consideration. The activity professional tries to anticipate how these symptoms will affect a resident's response in group activities and how other residents will respond when these symptoms occur. For example, a resident who is combative has the potential for striking out at other residents. This resident requires special monitoring if he/she is placed in a group to determine if this is a valid safety issue during group activities or if the behavior only occurs in specific situations such as ADL care.

A comparison of the activity assessment with sections of the MDS and the related RAPs helps to verify emotional conditions. A broader understanding of a resident's current reactions is gained, and approaches can be designed to modify and/or prevent mood and behavior problems. For example, an activity professional discovers that Ms. Hagerty responds positively to individual and group activities with no signs of distress during the last seven days, but the MDS indicates she has experienced distress within the last 30 days (MDS Section H). The activity professional seeks more information about when and how often this happens. It is found that no distress symptoms have occurred since admission, but she experienced significant tearfulness and agitation in the hospital as a result of feeling useless and bored. Since Ms. Hagerty is responding positively to activity programs, it is particularly important to consistently involve her in activity pursuits to prevent or decrease the possibility of a reoccurrence of distress.

Outcomes in emotional functioning can be objectively measured by using the MDS as a tool to note changes during the resident's stay in the facility. MDS Sections G, H and I show trends in progress or deterioration. For example, a male resident's initial MDS indicates that he is not at ease interacting with others (MDS Section G). One year later, the MDS shows this is no longer a problem, indicating a positive emotional outcome. If, at a later date, this resident again becomes ill at ease with others, the activity professional looks at the impact of recent changes in functioning and reviews the approaches that helped him overcome this problem in the past.

The MDS in conjunction with the activity care plan presents a picture of progress or deterioration. This picture can be used to target workable approaches based on a resident's response patterns. Using this strategy optimizes the potential for positive outcomes over time.

Withdrawal from past interests is a common symptom of emotional decline. This problem is indicated most often by a refusal to participate in facility activities and a lack of current interests. In the author's experience, emotional withdrawal is perhaps one of the most difficult behaviors to resolve. Residents who frequently refuse to attend group activities and/or participate in individual activities need to be carefully assessed to determine whether this behavior reflects a lifelong pattern or a shift in the recent past. If it has happened along with the aging process or other functioning changes, this behavior indicates a problem in emotional functioning. While solutions are not easily found, persistence is perhaps the most valuable tool. Documenting "refuses to attend" notes the behavior but does not indicate the end of the inquiry. Searching for clues that lead to the reengagement of the resident in former activity pursuits is the constant goal of the activity "detective." Assessment, adaptation and new approaches often yield a viable solution over time.

In a period when residents' rights are emerging as a critical aspect of resident care, the activity professional must be careful to recognize rights without overlooking significant emotional problems. While residents should not be forced to attend activities, new and creative approaches can be developed on an ongoing basis to gain a resident's interest. Restoring meaning to the last stage of a resident's life is a constant pursuit.

Social Assessment

Social functioning is examined by reviewing the diagnoses, evaluating current and past support systems, comparing current responses with past life patterns, and checking the related MDS sections. Psychiatric and medical diagnoses provide initial information about how a resident may interact with others. A resident with paranoia is not a candidate for large group activities until he/she feels comfortable with one-on-one relationships and small groups. A resident who has recently suffered a stroke and has aphasia may have difficulty maintaining and/or developing friendships due to communication deficits. In both of these examples, the diagnosis provides a framework for further exploration as the other assessment material is gathered.

SOCIAL ASSESSMENT	
Review:	Diagnoses
Evaluate:	Current and Past Support Systems
Compare:	Current Responses with Past Life Patterns
Analyze:	MDS Sections

Support systems include family, religious affiliation, organizational memberships, and friends. Refer to the activity therapy assessment form (Figure 6.1c) to see how these have been incorporated. Each system is examined for the role it plays in the resident's life. Once this is understood, the activity program can offer approaches that increase the supportive value of relationships.

The activity care plan is an avenue for assuring that the resident's relationship with family members is an optimal one. Since activity programs offer a familiar atmosphere, residents and family members who participate in activities together find it easier to maintain customary roles. The support provided by family members is often assumed to be positive. When this is not the case, it should be anticipated. Family members may visit frequently but also engage in arguments with the resident, causing the resident to have increased feelings of isolation. In this case, the activity intervention may include having family members attend social events with the resident where arguments are less likely to occur.

For many residents, religion has been one of the most valuable lifelong activities and the church or synagogue, etc., has been the most important institution in their lives. Religious beliefs may give them a sense of well-being in this life as well as hope for life after death. The activity professional evaluates the meaning religion holds for each resident and designs a plan that supports these beliefs. Residents sometimes have lost contact with their church due to extended illness. If it is not possible to locate church members who know the resident, finding a minister or other church members from the same denomination to visit is an alternative approach. Facilitating the resident's continued participation in specific religious activities also is explored. For example, a resident may be asked to make items for a church's or synagogue's bazaar or a committee could meet at the facility to accommodate the resident's attendance.

Organizational memberships and community involvement also are examined. Residents are offered opportunities to continue a similar level of interest in these areas in the facility. Raising money for community projects, volunteering to assist other residents, attending service club meetings in or out of the facility, and participating in intergenerational programs are a few examples of activity programs that promote residents' continued relationships with the community.

Peer relationships are a key to any individual's social health. Friends from the community are one of the most important links a resident can have for maintaining a positive image. Some residents have many lifelong friends; however, these friends also may suffer from illnesses or find it difficult to visit for other reasons, e.g., lack of transportation or fear of institutions. The activity professional explores these situations for possible interventions. A volunteer is assigned to help a resident write letters and make phone calls to friends. A resident's friends are invited to special events and transportation is arranged through community services. Some residents are new to the community and do not have many acquaintances. In this case, introducing the resident to other residents or community members with similar interests is a viable approach.

Knowledge about a resident's prior living arrangement is helpful in understanding a resident's responses, determining past support systems, and involving this support in the current situation. Note that "Living Arrangement Prior to Facility Placement" is included on Part 3 of the assessment form (Figure 6.1c). This is examined during the assessment interview along with other support system information. Jane Smith, whose assessment is illustrated, lived independently prior to her hospitalization. Having recently lived alone, she now finds herself living around other people twenty-four hours a day and is dependent on some of these people for meeting her needs. Issues of privacy and control are important to her. She does not cooperate when her personal care is provided because she resents the loss of independence and lack of privacy. She refuses involvement in group activities because she doesn't want others to see her dependency and it feels like an invasion of what privacy she has left. Ms. Smith is more comfortable when a friend attends activities with her and when activities are provided in her room on a one-on-one basis.

A comparison of current socialization with past life patterns reveals lifelong characteristics and current needs. If it is found that changes have occurred, noting when this happened suggests the cause and solutions. For example, a female resident who attended the senior citizen center weekly until undergoing a recent fall now has a decrease in her social contacts. This decrease is probably due to her current physical status and related changes in her routine. The therapeutic intervention primarily centers on preventing a continuation of this decline by providing opportunities for socialization with other residents and asking her friends to visit frequently.

A resident's desire to attend the facility's group activities is compared to his/her past lifestyle regarding involvement in social functions. A resident who was quite active socially until one or two years ago now refuses to attend group activities; this current response indicates that the resident is withdrawing from a previous behavior pattern. Initially, the resident may have become isolated due to decreased opportunities for socialization. Transportation barriers, death of close friends, and other causes could have led to fewer contacts. The resident may now fear socialization and try to isolate himself/herself. Approaches involve a gradual increase of social interaction by starting with one-on-one visitation and gradually progressing to groups.

Observations of social interactions is another key factor in assessment and care plan design. Facial expressions, tone of voice, gestures and actual words offer clues about how to maintain or improve social health. Watching residents in a variety of settings is helpful to a more comprehensive understanding. For example, Ms. Smith smiles and relaxes when she is asked about her family members, church choir director, and neighbors. She becomes tense when she is in the hallway among people she does not know. The most effective approaches to increasing her socialization include involving her in activities with familiar people.

Sections of the MDS that relate to social functioning include Sections III—Customary Routine, C—Communication/Hearing Patterns, G—Psychosocial Well-being, H—Mood and Behavior Patterns and I—Activity Pursuit Patterns. Cycle of Daily Events and Involvement Patterns in Section III are particularly relevant. This section targets the previous year rather than the last seven days. If a resident spent most of his/her time alone or watching TV. (III—Item 1e), did not usually attend church, temple, synagogue, etc., (III—Item 1r) and was not involved in group activities (III—Item 1u), this data indicates few social contacts. If limited socialization is a lifelong pattern, this is a preferred routine. If limited socialization appeared with a deteriorating physical status during the last year, this resident is a candidate for

gradually increasing socialization. If the pattern is well established, the change is expected to be gradual.

Section C—Communication/Hearing Patterns identifies basic communication skills and deficits. Residents who have hearing and communication deficits sometimes isolate themselves from others by refusing to attend group activities and/or refusing individual contacts. Learning to communicate with this type of resident effectively and teaching others these communication skills are primary approaches to consider.

Section G—Psychosocial Well-Being provides a broad perspective of social functioning. "Sense Of Initiative/Involvement" looks at positive interaction and involvement patterns. "Unsettled Relationships" gives a potentially contrasting picture related to conflicts, isolation, and loss. This can help the activity professional identify strengths as well as anticipate poor outcomes. For example, Ms. White's MDS has every item of Section G Item 1 checked. The only item checked under Section G Item 2 is "f" "Recent loss of close family member/friend." This loss alerts the activity professional to the potential for a bad outcome. Further investigation shows that Ms. White had a friendship with another resident, Mr. Long. Mr. Long died a few days prior to the completion of the MDS. While Ms. White is not yet showing signs of a decrease in her social involvement, it is important to establish approaches that assure she has opportunities to grieve.

The author is aware of a case where a facility's staff did not recognize a resident's need to grieve due to outward signs of adjustment to the loss. Over a period of six months, the resident began to physically deteriorate because of a decrease in appetite and a desire to stay in bed most of the time. Her physical deterioration continued until the resident was encouraged to talk about her loss and begin the grieving process. Besides talking about the death, the grieving process for this resident included obtaining a copy of her friend's obituary, establishing a memorial fund, and collecting pictures of the friend's involvement in facility activity programs. This example illustrates the need for activity professionals to understand normal reactions to death and to provide opportunities to work through the grieving process. When these reactions are not apparent, a resident may be inappropriately coping by avoiding discussions of feelings. The consequences of not dealing with a loss can lead to severe physical problems and even death.

Sections G, H, and I contain many other items that potentially affect a resident's social functioning. Conflicts with roommates and/or family members, sad or anxious moods, and problem behaviors (Section G and H) are examples. Time awake, preferred activity settings, and activity preferences (Section I) are clues about a resident's opportunities for social involvement.

Cognitive Assessment

Assessing cognitive functioning involves reviewing the diagnoses, evaluating the level of orientation and memory, and analyzing the related MDS Sections. Before reviewing the diagnoses, it is important to understand the four primary conditions that cause disorientation. Delirium comprises a group of symptoms including reduced ability to maintain attention, disorganized thinking, incoherent speech, sensory misperceptions, and disorientation (Dorlands, 1988). The delirious person shows a reduced level of consciousness while the person with dementia is clearly awake. People with dementia also can suffer from delirium. (Mace, 1981) Residents sometimes suffer from delirium with common acute illnesses such as urinary tract infections and pneumonia. In fact, it can be one of the first presenting symptoms of these conditions.

Acute/reversible dementia can be caused by hospital psychosis, thyroid disturbances and many other metabolic disruptions. On-set of delirium and acute/reversible dementia usually is rapid. Symptoms are usually alleviated by treating the underlying cause.

Causes for chronic dementias include Alzheimer's disease, strokes, Parkinson's disease, AIDS, alcoholism, and other more rare causes, such as Huntington's disease. The onset of Alzheimer's disease usually is gradual and continues to progress over time. Dementia caused by a stroke may be acute or chronic. The onset occurs with the incidence of the stroke or strokes. The symptoms progress in step-like fashion. Some stroke residents will maintain the same level of orientation with no deterioration for a long period of time if another stroke does not occur. For the other chronic dementias, the progression differs according to the specific dementia.

Depression in the elderly often shows many symptoms that mimic dementia. In these cases, successful treatment of depression resolves the disorientation and memory problems. This disorder is sometimes called pseudodementia.

Despite the diagnosis, the severity of the symptoms can vary dramatically. The effect these symptoms have on resident's abilities is observed during interviews and activity participation. The assessment targets the level of orientation and its effect on activity involvement.

COGNITIVE ASSESSMENT

Review:	**Diagnoses**
Evaluate:	**Orientation**
Evaluate:	**Recent and Remote Memory**
Analyze:	**MDS Sections**

"Orientation "is a term referring to a person's understanding of four areas: situation, person, time, and place. Assessment begins by determining a person's ability to relate to these four areas. When interviewing a resident, probes such as "Tell me about your current situation" can illicit the necessary information. For residents who are unable to speak, observation is used; examples include "resident participates in ADLs and attends and participates in activity pursuits (orientation to situation)", "resident responds to name and facial expression (orientation to person)", "resident heads toward dining room at lunchtime (orientation to time)" and "resident finds his/her room (orientation to place)."

Orientation is a broad area that requires specific descriptions to reveal abilities as well as deficits. Generic labels such as "Disorientation" are appropriate for a problem list, but they are inadequate for pinpointing cognitive status. How the resident's level of disorientation affects activity pursuit patterns is the goal of the evaluation. For example, Ms. Jones takes the hand of familiar residents during activities. She finds her room with verbal and physical prompts. She is frequently concerned about paying for her room but forgets this worry during music activities or one-on-one talks about her garden. This example shows that Ms. Jones suffers from cognitive deficits but still maintains many orientation skills. She is able to pay attention to a task at hand if it is pleasurable and maintains positive relationships though she may not be able to give specific names. Notice how the specificity of this description emphasizes what Ms. Jones *can* accomplish.

Memory skills are tested by asking items that require remote and recent recall of information, e.g., "How long have you been here?" (recent) "How many years of school did you attend?" (remote). These questions usually fall naturally into the assessment interview when discussing past and current interests. The information a resident provides is compared with the social and medical histories, the MDS, and other assessment data. If there is a disparity, further evaluation is necessary to determine if the record is inaccurate or if the resident has some memory deficits.

MDS Appendix A—Section B—Cognitive Patterns has additional information. Indicators Of Delirium—Periodic Disordered Thinking/Awareness (Item 5, page 117) is an area that merits special attention. It is the author's experience that many of these symptoms are first noticed during a resident's participation in activity pursuits. They are of particular importance since they can indicate serious acute illnesses. The activity professional needs to routinely observe residents for any sudden variations in thinking or participation patterns and communicate these changes to the nursing staff.

Activity Pursuit Patterns

Understanding activity pursuit patterns requires the recognition of each resident's individuality in relation to a variety of factors. Some of these were covered in the previous materials. Chapter 8's discussion of outcomes will illustrate additional assessment criteria which, due to their personal nature, usually cannot be evaluated until the resident lives in the facility for a period of time. This section will consider four activity pursuit evaluation areas: level of activity participation, individual and/or group activity preferences, type of activity preferences, and the personal meaning activity pursuits hold.

ACTIVITY PURSUIT ASSESSMENT CRITERIA

- **Level of Participation**
- **Individual or Group Preferences**
- **Type of Preferences**
- **Meaning of Pursuits**

Activity pursuit assessment examines the routine level of activity participation and identifies preferences for individual and/or group participation. Level of participation refers to frequency as well as the amount of physical or emotional energy an individual invests. Activity patterns vary widely from one person to another. Some people prefer a busy lifestyle when almost all of their time is involved in activities such as work, sports, or volunteer commitments. Others enjoy mostly sedentary activities such as watching television, riding in a car, or reading. Some people pursue their preferences alone while others seek constant companionship.

Most activity pursuit patterns involve a combination of varied levels of participation and solitary and group experiences. For example, Ms. Jacobs indicates an interest in tasks related to her career as a homemaker and her role as a church member. She describes her life as having a relatively slow pace. She has never cared for being rushed. She says, "It took me nearly a year to complete a quilt, much slower than my neighbors. I always preferred doing my handwork alone and only occasionally attended quilting bees. Church was different. I hadn't missed attending a church service or committee meeting in my life until I got sick." These statements indicate that Ms. Jacobs has an interest in quilting, but prefers to participate in this hobby on an infrequent basis by herself and, on rare occasions, in a group. In contrast, her interest in church activities involves frequent group participation. Offering her regular opportunities to continue her church-related groups will maintain her previous routine.

Identifying preferences with regard to a general activity category, for example, gardening or music, is only the first clue in discovering the range of a resident's interests. Effective activity approaches are dependent on more specific information. For example, when assessing music tastes, it is essential to determine the specific kind(s) of music a resident prefers, e.g., classical, jazz, country, or gospel. Research has shown that positive responses to music depend a great deal on an elderly person's familiarity with, and like for, specific types of music (Gibbons,

1977). A resident may in fact have a negative response to music which is not a personal preference. Hard rock music, a type of music generally not preferred by the elderly, may cause agitation. Some other aspects related to music are whether the resident has participated in music as a professional or amateur musician or whether the resident has primarily been an observer/listener of music. This specificity of data is imperative to matching residents' interests.

The final, and perhaps most important, area to assess is the meaning a resident gives to a particular activity. Collecting information on the areas mentioned previously (level of activity participation, individual and/or group activity preferences, and type of activity preferences) furnishes clues regarding the meaning activity pursuits hold for the resident. To obtain a complete picture, this additional factor must be considered. The meaning a resident gives to an activity pursuit is often reflected in the individual's experience of an activity as work, recreation, spiritual, and/or creative expression. There are many factors which may influence this view, childhood experiences, special talents, family history, historical events, or individual personalities. All of these will not be examined in this context; however, material on some of the main areas will be presented.

Aging cohorts refers to the tendency for people born around the same time period to share common behavioral, attitudinal, and value characteristics. They are key factors to consider in determining the resident's experience of a particular activity (Walz, 1988). For example, while the meaning an individual gives to a particular activity may be reflected in the amount of time spent in pursuing an interest, this data may take on new meaning when it is tempered with aging cohort factors.

Most residents have spent a majority of their time pursuing a career. Since the work ethic has been shown to be very strong in persons who were born before World War II

(Walz, 1988), residents in this cohort may respond positively to work-related activities. It is important to note that these residents are likely to view these activities as serious responsibilities. Another specific example is elderly women in some parts of the country who have quilted most of their lives. Today, quilting is viewed more as a creative and/or recreational activity, but many elderly women experience it as work since it has been traditionally done out of need, not for leisure. For a resident who views quilting as work, participation in a quilting project may only be desirable if the resident knows the quilt will be used for a specific purpose. Many of today's elderly have experienced activity pursuits in the context of work. The activity professional must be especially sensitive to this aging cohort in the development of therapeutic programming.

A resident's individual experiences of an activity pursuit may not relate to aging cohorts but simply to a resident's personal choices and/or talents. For example, a resident who showed a great deal of musical talent as a child and who pursued a career as a professional musician may view music as creatively- and work-oriented. Yet, a resident who has primarily participated in music as an amateur in community bands may view music as creative and recreational. For the professional musician, music programs may need to be highly structured and goal-oriented, while the amateur musician may prefer playing an instrument and/or singing in less structured groups, i.e., sing-a-longs. All of these meanings have particular significance to activity programming.

Maslow's Hierarchy of Needs

Knowledge about the resident's functioning and activity pursuit patterns provides a backdrop for establishing the overall effect the present circumstances are having on the individual. The resident's progress, or lack

thereof, in maintaining a satisfying life in the context of the current situation should be revealed as part of the assessment process. A convenient way of conceptualizing the resident's overall outlook is to use Maslow's Hierarchy of Needs.

Abraham Maslow (1908-1970) believed that human beings are constantly seeking a higher level of personal development and functioning. He suggested that human needs vary from basic physiological requirements to fully integrated peaks of human behavior which he termed "self-actualization." His Hierarchy of Needs (Figure 6.3) states that the lowest, or most basic, unmet need dominates the attention and energy of an individual. As more primitive needs are consistently met, human beings search for "fulfillment" of their potential at a higher "need level,": "Man demonstrates in his own nature a pressure toward fuller and fuller Being, more and more perfect actualization of his humanness in exactly the same naturalistic, scientific sense that an acorn may be said to be 'pressing toward' being an oak tree" (Maslow, 1968).

Each person experiences this hierarchy in a different way. It is not intended to be used as a narrow definition of human existence, but as a tool to help more effectively assess residents' reactions to their current circumstances. Some people stay at a basic need level for an extended period of time while others are near the lower end for only a brief period before regaining their previous status. Residents who are overwhelmed with the trauma of entering the facility may express constant concern for physiological needs, e.g., "When will supper come?" and safety/shelter needs, e.g., "Where is my room?" "I can't leave this place because someone might steal my possessions". The length of time at which these concerns continue as the sole interest of the resident depends on the interventions used, the resident's response, the disease process, and other factors, such as past lifestyle.

A devastating experience can send a person down the hierarchy to the lower, more primitive need levels even though this individual may have been directed toward and may have attained a high level. For example, Mr. Hartman, an elderly gentleman who has prided himself on being able to live independently at the age of 91, breaks a hip and enters a long-term care facility for rehabilitation. Upon admission, he is disoriented, frequently asking about mealtimes (physiological need) and if he has a place to spend the night (safety need). Once he has been assured of his physiological and safety needs, he begins to form relationships with the staff and other residents (love need). He gradually becomes less confused and starts seeking ways to regain his self-respect. He asks to help deliver the mail. This volunteer job of mail delivery is more than a way to occupy time; it is a way of coping with his life's circumstances, a tool for gaining his self-esteem. Unless the activity professional realizes the meaning this task holds for him, Mr. Hartman could lose his recently regained self-worth if the job is inadvertently given to someone else.

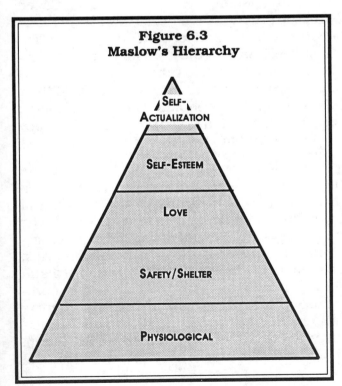

**Figure 6.3
Maslow's Hierarchy**

SELF-ACTUALIZATION

SELF-ESTEEM

LOVE

SAFETY/SHELTER

PHYSIOLOGICAL

Other people have incredible abilities to rebound from traumatic situations with no or limited assistance. For example, during a conversation with Chloe, a seventy-five-year-old friend of the author, Chloe described a particularly difficult time in her life. Chloe was in the hospital recuperating from a severely fractured hip. She had been hospitalized numerous times over the past few months and was told her possibility for complete recovery was uncertain. At the same time, her husband, Thomas, was in the intensive care unit at the same hospital, expected to die of heart failure. One evening, the night nurse said to Chloe, "I believe that Thomas may die tonight. I think you should come and say good-bye." Chloe immediately went with the nurse to see her husband. In relating the events to the author, Chloe stated, "Do you know what that nurse did when we got to Thomas' room? She pulled up a chair beside the bed for me and *then* she pulled up a chair for herself. Did she not think I might have something to say to Thomas which I didn't want her to hear?" Chloe hesitated and then stated with a laugh, "I considered this situation for a few moments. I thought of saying: 'Thomas, this is a confession, there have been many men in my life.'" The author commented that this might have awakened the nurse to the need for Chloe and Thomas to have some privacy. Chloe replied, "What? If I had really said that, she would have stayed all night, and I never would have gotten rid of her!"

This example illustrates how a person who was overcome with concerns for her own physical needs due to a fractured hip (physiological needs) was able to quickly move up the hierarchy from the lowest level to self-esteem. This move was exemplified in her ability to regain a sense of humor. Chloe's attitude toward life indicated an ability to effectively cope in extremely difficult circumstances.

Residents at each level have behavior patterns and/or characteristics that are helpful in understanding where they fit on the hierarchy. As with all assessment processes, each individual's past history with regard to having their needs met plays a role in expected results. New admissions like Mr. Hartman, mid-stage Alzheimer's residents, and residents who suffer from severe pain are examples of residents who may be at the physiological level for brief periods, usually until they are reassured and their basic needs are met. All the energy these residents expend in conversations and actions primarily centers on physiological needs.

Residents who stay at the physiological level for extended periods are not generally common even in a facility primarily caring for the critically ill. These residents usually do not indicate any awareness of their surroundings and show no responses to human contact. Awareness is limited to their body's basic needs, i.e., comfort, food and thirst. The body is their total environment. Residents who are in a coma or who are in the end stage of Alzheimer's disease are examples.

Residents who are seeking safety are usually fearful and are constantly asking questions related to safety and shelter, e.g., "Where will I sleep tonight?", "How will I pay for this meal?" and "Where will I get my shower?" Some of the residents who tend to exhibit these symptoms are new admissions and mid-stage Alzheimer's (as noted under physiological), the blind, and oriented residents who are dependent on the staff for most of their ADL care. These residents often have short attention spans and find it difficult to form relationships because they are consumed with their need to feel safe. Staying at this level is usually a temporary condition once interventions are employed. A resident who has dementia, for instance, may feel insecure at all times during the initial admission and later, when the facility and staff are more familiar, concern for safety may taper off to an occasional occurrence.

An oriented resident who is dependent on the staff for most of his/her ADL care may become consumed with whether these needs will be met. This resident may respond by expressing anxiety about the staff's competence to meet his/her needs. When the staff consistently respond on a timely basis, the anxiety will be reduced. Residents who are seeking love often demand attention. These residents may ring the call bell frequently without specific reasons. Residents who need love will seek any form of attention, negative or positive. Even residents who receive frequent family visits may feel alienated from their families due to lifelong or recent conflicts. Meeting the need for love often takes a longer period than physiological or safety needs since relationships require time to develop.

Residents who are seeking self-esteem are seldom completely satisfied with their situation and express insecurity regarding their abilities to complete tasks they are capable of finishing. These residents may be active participants in activity programs, but they do not seem to be reaching their maximum potential and are often dissatisfied with the programs offered. They do not make choices easily and feel a lack of control over their lives. As with the need for love, attaining a sense of self-esteem takes a longer period of time. Residents need to be assured that their choices will be honored. They may observe other residents making decisions before they feel comfortable to do the same.

Residents seeking self-actualization are generally self-assured and are engaged in a life review which examines their past and attempts to make a coherent picture of its meaning. These residents spend a great deal of time reminiscing not only about memories, but about the meaning of the memories and how it relates to their present life's circumstances. They may participate in activities which they have wanted to pursue all their lives but for which they never found the time. Residents who reach this level tend to control how this need will be met and will request what is necessary to attain their goals. For some, the process is a solitary one while others wish to share their experiences.

Assessment of Incongruence

The MDS and all assessment components are constantly reviewed and compared to uncover any areas that seem incongruent with normal reactions to difficult human situations, e.g., losses, conflicts, changes, or normal desires for meeting human needs. The previous case of a resident who had experienced a loss but continued to interact with others as if nothing had occurred illustrated the importance of this assessment principle. The activity professional should investigate whether the assessment data makes sense given the resident's current situation.

The author reviewed a female resident's chart and found she had suffered a recent debilitating stroke. She had lost all speech and was no longer able to perform any ADLs without assistance. The MDS Section H— Mood and Behavior Patterns (Appendix A, indicated she had no Verbal Expression of Distress (Item 1a) and no Demonstrated Signs of Mental Distress (Item 1b-g). It is highly unlikely that such a complete change in physical status would not trigger an emotional reaction. The stroke may have impaired her ability to express a response, and she may actually have been suffering from depression and/or felt that her physiological and safety needs were not being met. Another possibility is that the MDS did not contain the item describing her reaction. Any of these types of scenarios merit further probing.

The author worked with another resident who had suffered a stroke and the loss of his wife almost simultaneously. In evaluating the resident, the author found that he did not maintain eye contact and in fact kept his head down almost all the time. When asked questions such as, "Are you doing okay?" he would reply, "Yes." The author asked that he be assessed by a physician to determine the viability of an anti-depressant regime. The physician interviewed the resident and documented that the "resident denies depression; no treatment necessary." This assessment, unfortunately, overlooked the obvious withdrawn behavior and poor judgment which are both symptoms of depression (Fry, 1986).

Assessment of incongruency is a constant strategy for improving comprehensive understanding. It requires general knowledge about common functioning problems and normal behavioral patterns coupled with information about individual resident's experiences. When the resident's outcome is poor and unexpected, exploration of disparities in the assessment can provide necessary clues to positively changing the results of care planning.

Strengths and Weaknesses

The exploration of functioning, activity pursuit patterns, needs, and incongruence uncovers strengths and weaknesses. Strengths are potential coping mechanisms for dealing with the current situation. They are reflected in past achievements and in abilities which have enabled the resident to meet life's opportunities and challenges.

Weaknesses are the primary barriers to a satisfactory activity pursuit pattern. They are the accumulation of functioning deficits and patterns that interfere with quality of life experiences. Identification of these areas reveals the hurdles standing in the way of resident progress.

Both strengths and weaknesses depict strategies for creating a workable activity care plan. For example, a withdrawn elderly woman is admitted. Her history shows that she raised ten children. In discussing this with her, the activity professional, Mr. West, discovers that she has always been proud of her ability to manage such a large family. She expresses sadness over her lost role. When observing her outside her room, Mr. West notices that she assists other residents who cannot propel their own wheelchairs. She continues to nurture others as she did her many children. This desire to care for others can be tapped as a resource to help restore her sense of pride and decrease her withdrawal. For example, she may be matched with a disoriented resident who needs companionship.

The final step of the assessment is to summarize strengths and weaknesses into brief terms that direct the care plan's content. The Strengths and Weaknesses section of the assessment form provides brief, general descriptions (Figure 6.1e). More detailed information is already clearly identified in the body of the assessment. Ms. Smith's assessment lists "Limited Current Involvement in Activity Pursuits" as a weakness. MDS Section I and several statements on the assessment form verify this conclusion.

Strengths include past and current activity pursuits and current functioning abilities. Identifying past strengths is particularly important for residents who have few current abilities since it provides a building block for interventions. Refer again to the assessment form (Figure 6.1e). Ms. Smith's strengths are identified in the areas of activity interests and social, cognitive and physical functioning.

The first weakness identified is the need dominating the resident's life. This weakness is listed first because the need consuming the attention and energy of the resident must be resolved before other weaknesses can be effectively addressed. "Feels Unloved/Needs Attention" is listed on the assessment form (Figure 6.1e) as Ms. Smith's primary weakness. The need for love engrosses her to the point that she cannot focus on improving her mobility, communication or activity involvement. Once she feels a greater sense of companionship, she will be able to concentrate on other areas.

The other listed weaknesses are the most significant functional deficits and activity pursuit problems. Examples of functional deficits include disorientation, withdrawal, low endurance, isolation, and poor adjustment to facility placement. Limited current involvement covers a wide range of activity pursuit problems. If more specificity is desired, the following items could be considered: few interests, limited setting preferences, prefers more or different activities, refuses participation in facility programs, and limited community involvement. The author recommends that three or four weaknesses be identified; as a general rule, this number will encompass the primary areas of concern which can be reasonably impacted within the first two to three months of a resident's stay.

Summary

Knowledge of common functioning problems, needs, and normal reactions to the aging process coupled with activity assessment principles pinpoints discrepancies and uncovers areas requiring further evaluation. This information is applied to the unique functioning abilities and deficits, characteristics, and lifelong patterns of each individual and reveals the breadth of strengths and weaknesses a resident possesses. Once these steps are achieved, preventative and restorative measures are implemented, and a plan for resident fulfillment is set in motion.

Assessment is ongoing. The specificity of the information obtained is crucial to individualized programming. Collecting this data only begins with the initial assessment. Time and the resident's condition may limit the amount of data that can be gathered in the beginning. The activity care plan's unremitting success depends on the first assessment and the activity professional's ability to continue obtaining clues throughout the resident's stay in the facility. This discovery happens through routine consultation with the resident and observation of responses to a variety of activity services.

Case Examples

The following case examples are designed to illustrate how assessment data can be used to restore activity pursuit patterns. All are based on actual case histories. The names and some of the specifics have been changed to assure confidentiality.

Ms. Smith

The narrative for Ms. Smith's case example is in Chapter 4, page 23. The reader may want to review this text as well as the assessment form before reading the next section.

Assessment Conclusions and Actions Taken

Ms. Smith's dependency on others for tasks of which she is capable and her attention-seeking behavior are signs that she feels unloved. Even though her family is supportive, Ms. Smith spends most of her time with strangers, her caregivers. Developing approaches to help Ms. Smith feel more loved by the staff and others is a logical starting point for her activity care plan. Since Deanna already has a relationship with Ms. Smith, Deanna is an excellent resource. Deanna accompanies Ms. Smith to one of the facility's music programs. Deanna's presence is reassuring to Ms. Smith and helps her gain enough confidence to begin singing with the other residents. Over a period of time, the activity professional, Ms. Frost, is able to form a relationship with Ms. Smith. Eventually, Ms. Smith starts attending music activities at Ms. Frost's request without needing Deanna's companionship.

Results of her increased activity involvement spill over into other areas. She becomes more trusting of the staff with regard to taking showers, decreases the use of her call bell, and increases her independence in ADLs. Once Ms. Smith feels loved, approaches are implemented to increase her self-esteem.

Ms. Smith becomes an active member of the resident choir, singing solos and helping to choose the music. At this point, Ms. Smith is encouraged by Ms. Frost to learn to propel her wheelchair. She is hesitant at first, but her renewed self-confidence and desire to get to activities motivates her to gradually become independent in wheelchair mobility.

It is important to note that once goals have been achieved, accomplishments must be maintained through ongoing monitoring of a resident's condition and development of new approaches as indicated. At a later point, Ms. Smith suffers a sudden onset of blindness. She immediately begins to show signs of dependency by refusing to get out of bed or attend activities. Ms. Frost becomes concerned that Ms. Smith will lose her restored sense of self-esteem if this new problem and new signs of dependency are not addressed immediately. Ms. Frost institutes a new plan of action within a few days. A performance of the resident choir is scheduled within a few weeks; this gives Ms. Smith a positive focus in her life despite the physical setback. In addition, another resident is assigned to give Ms. Smith verbal instructions as she propels her wheelchair through the hallways to activities. This approach is initially observed by Ms. Frost to assure that it is a safe and reasonable approach. These two interventions are effective in helping Ms. Smith maintain her self-esteem and wheelchair mobility.

Mr. Fredrick

In the following case study, note the sequence in which the approaches are applied which is directly relevant to the effectiveness of the plan.

Mr. Fredrick is an oriented 70-year-old man who is placed in a long-term care facility as a result of a stroke which limits his ability to care for himself independently. He initially receives physical and occupational therapy and is discharged from these programs since it is determined that he has reached his maximum potential. He continues to need help with transfers and dressing. He rolls his wheelchair without assistance and has good use of one arm and hand and partial use of his other arm and hand. He participated in a restorative feeding program where he learned to feed himself without assistance; however, his eating habits remain poor. Most residents refuse to sit next to him during mealtime because of his unsightly habits. His eating appears not to improve due to a lack of motivation rather than an inability to eat properly.

Mr. Fredrick frequently lashes out verbally and physically at the staff. Most of the staff members react to these outbursts by scolding Mr. Fredrick or ignoring the behavior as if they expect nothing better from him. He attends activities occasionally, but he frequently is rude to the activity professional, Ms. Karen Frost, as well as the other residents. Mr. Fredrick is essentially isolated from any meaningful relationships with staff or residents. In addition, his only son visits just one time a year.

His former occupation is farming. His only other known past interests are church and music. He refuses to give specific information about either of these interests. He states that religion is important to him. He frequently expounds on his religious beliefs to others, usually by pointing out their faults. Mr. Fredrick does not know any ministers in the local area.

Assessment Conclusions and Actions Taken

Mr. Fredrick expends a great deal of energy getting the attention of the staff. Unfortunately, he mainly receives negative attention due to his aggressive behavior. Ms. Frost does not accurately identify Mr. Fredrick's need initially due to her own harsh feelings toward him. It is difficult for her to see beyond his inappropriate behavior.

Once it is obvious that Mr. Fredrick feels a total sense of abandonment, Ms. Frost realizes that more assessment clues are needed before effective approaches can be implemented. It is discovered that Mr. Fredrick was abused as a child, and he abused his only son. This behavior resulted in their poor relationship. Because Mr. Fredrick has never known much affection in the sense of physical touch and a friendly manner, Ms. Frost begins to search for ways to demonstrate to Mr. Fredrick that he is loved in a manner which will be understood by him. Ms. Frost discontinues any attempts to scold Mr. Fredrick for poor behavior and begins to focus solely on forming a relationship with him.

One of Mr. Fredrick's strengths is his strong determination. This strength is often exhibited by a very "grouchy" exterior. Ms. Frost uses this personality characteristic in a cheerful manner in addressing Mr. Fredrick. Ms. Frost begins this relationship by inviting him to activities on a regular basis.

When he replies in a gruff manner, she refers to Mr. Fredrick as the "world's greatest grouch," teasing him about his lack of a smile. Ms. Frost observes him carefully to assure the right approach is being used. Mr. Fredrick responds by grinning and laughing. Gradually, other residents and staff begin to give Mr. Fredrick attention by cheerfully noting his grumpy personality. Every time he enters a room, he gets positive attention. His combativeness and verbal abusiveness are almost completely eliminated.

Once Mr. Fredrick feels loved, his self-esteem can be increased. He asks to play a specific role in the Christmas play which involves the biblical story of Mary and Joseph making their trip to the stable. In keeping with Mr. Fredrick's character, he asks to play the role of the Innkeeper. He observes, "Who else can turn Mary and Joseph away but the 'world's greatest grouch'?" Again Mr. Fredrick receives positive attention and his self-esteem is increased because he has a sense of responsibility and is able to successfully complete a task of his choice.

A couple of months after these approaches are implemented, Mr. Fredrick verbally lashes out at another resident during an activity program. Ms. Frost firmly explains to Mr. Fredrick that this behavior will not be tolerated and that she expects more from him. He is quite angry but returns that afternoon to apologize. No further such incidents occur. It is possible for Ms. Frost to take this firm approach at this point in time because Mr. Fredrick respects her opinion. Before a relationship was formed, Ms. Frost's thoughts about his behavior were of no consequence to Mr. Fredrick.

Ms. Melbeth

Ms. Melbeth is a disoriented 80-year-old woman who is admitted to a long-term care facility because of her increasingly unpredictable behavior. During the past two to three years, Ms. Melbeth has shown poor judgment with regard to managing her financial affairs; frequently she did not pay her bills and withdrew large amounts of money that are now unaccounted for. She was recently diagnosed as having Alzheimer's disease. The severity of her disorientation is moderate; she is able to carry on short conversations about her interests, her family and her feelings.

She ambulates independently and her physical endurance is good. Ms. Melbeth paces constantly, asking for reassurance regarding the environment. She frequently becomes lost. She is unable to stay for more than five minutes in a group activity. She feeds herself without hands-on assistance but needs reminders to focus her attention on her food. She is friendly but is isolated from others due to her short attention span, constant questioning and anxious affect.

Ms. Melbeth's activity assessment indicates she worked as a successful banker, raised a family of three, and was happily married until her husband's death. After her retirement, she remained active by doing volunteer work and joining social clubs. She sang in community choirs and church choirs most of her life. Ms. Melbeth always felt a sense of security and love; her work achievements and many interests provided her with a high sense of self-esteem. Ms. Melbeth enjoyed the companionship of others, especially on a one-on-one basis.

Assessment Conclusions and Actions Taken

Ms. Melbeth currently feels a tremendous amount of concern related to her safety/ shelter needs. She does not recognize the staff and cannot find her room. This insecurity needs to be addressed to help her adjust to the facility and overcome her sense of anxiety. During Ms. Melbeth's initial stay, staff members work together to constantly reassure her that she has a room to sleep in and will be safe. She is provided with one-on-one activities and is gradually integrated into groups. It is noticed that Ms. Melbeth responds to people who touch her and speak in a friendly manner. During group programs, she is placed next to a resident who holds her hand and reassures her throughout the activity. Ms. Melbeth cannot remember this resident's name, but after a short period of time she demonstrates recognition by seeking a chair next to her without any prompting from the activity professional, Ms. Hartman. Ms. Melbeth also is placed next to the door so that she can easily leave if she is unable to tolerate the entire activity. Throughout the day, if Ms. Hartman sees that Ms. Melbeth is anxious or fearful, she takes a few moments to walk her to her room and comfort her, frequently mentioning the name of Ms. Melbeth's daughter because this name decreases her distress.

Ms. Melbeth is more adjusted to the facility after a few months and begins to participate in activities that increase her feelings of love and self-esteem. The section on tailored activities in Chapter 7 gives a specific example of how an activity is adapted to meet Ms. Melbeth's needs despite her short attention span.

7 PROGRAM DEVELOPMENT

Assessment lays out the necessary tools for creating activity programs. This assessment includes an evaluation of the common problems of the long-term care population and the specific needs of individual residents. The initial "core" activity program is based on what is known about the general health needs of a facility's current residents. This is a starting point for improving residents' physical, social, cognitive, and emotional functioning.

Once core programs are in place, they become progressively more tailored to individuals as a result of ongoing assessment. Distinctive resident preferences are increasingly apparent over time through communication and observations of participation in core programs. These responses are routinely monitored, and tailored approaches are implemented accordingly. The results of increasingly more individualized services continue to be tracked since residents' tastes and needs are constantly evolving. Activity program development like resident assessment is an unremitting process of change.

Core Activities

Implementation of core programs begins with the provision of activities that treat the primary functional areas. These activities include group programs and individual services. Poor nutritional intake is a common symptom of a physical functioning problem. A special homestyle breakfast provides food that is cooked in the resident's presence and stimulates an appetite, thus increasing physical functioning. Creative writing experiences or music appreciation classes increase cognitive functioning. Resident visiting committees offer opportunities for socialization and curb feelings of loneliness. A resident's participation in pet therapy or service work improves emotional functioning.

The specific core activities are chosen depending on the common interests of the residents living in a given facility. Programs are devised using these preferences to improve the functioning areas. If most of the activity assessments indicate an interest in cooking, this activity is considered a typical interest. A cooking activity is created to focus on social and cognitive functioning by encouraging residents to share recipes and reminisce about cooking. Another cooking activity increases physical functioning by having residents stir, chop and measure ingredients. Emotional functioning is enhanced when a resident participates in planning his/her own cooking project. Matching activities to common interests and functioning needs provide limitless program possibilities.

Core activities often are designed to address only one or two primary problems, but they can be adapted to provide a variety of benefits. For example, a daily exercise class is scheduled to improve the physical functioning of residents. Since the class involves a group of people, the residents also are afforded opportunities to socialize. The daily schedule and repetition of the exercises offers an effective treatment for withdrawal. A discussion of current events ensues during the class to stimulate cognitive functioning. Adapting activities so they address all four areas of functioning whenever possible is an efficient approach to service provision. Every program is reviewed to determine if it can be modified to expand its benefits for residents.

Development of core programs constitutes a fine balance between adapting the program to maximize results in functioning and providing a consistent structure. Consistency with regard to the program schedule, leadership style, and resident expectations reflects reliability to the participants. People respond positively to predictable situations because they reduce anxiety and build security and confidence. On the other hand, adaptability with regard to altering the program to enhance individual functioning signifies flexibility to the participants. Residents feel safe to express their abilities and preferences. Consistency that is rigid can stifle creativity just as adaptability that is uncontrolled can produce anxiety. The appropriate balance is determined by observing resident responses.

Mr. Connor, a resident who had been a caterer all his life and who continued to have a keen interest in fine cuisine, was admitted to a long-term care facility. His stay in the facility was to be short-term, probably four to six weeks. Ms. Frost, the activity professional, reviewed the activity calendar for programs matching his interest. She discovered that the annual fund-raising event would take place before his discharge. Ms. Frost asked Mr. Connor if he would make suggestions for catering this event. He was informed of the budget and time limits. Having been a businessman for forty years, he was quite familiar with such limitations and enthusiastically agreed to plan the menu. Mr. Connor experienced an increase in his emotional functioning by giving his assistance. The schedule for the event remained consistent; yet, the activity was adapted to maximize benefits.

Tailored Activities

Core activities are the foundation for an excellent activity program. However, if building stops at the foundation, the program will lack growth, individualization, and creativity. Core activities address general functioning, but they fall short of touching the depth of each person. Tailored activities are designed to highlight the possibilities of each resident's life. Developing activities with therapeutic relevance is accomplished by using Maslow's Hierarchy of Needs as an initial guideline and then examining supportive, maintenance and empowerment activity outcomes. This chapter will show how each need of the hierarchy is used to determine what activity criteria must be met to fulfill that need.

Physiological Needs

Basic physiological needs are satisfied by adequate nutritional intake, sensory stimulation, and a comfortable environment. A resident whose awareness does not go beyond physiological needs can be effectively served with activities that supplement these areas. Providing prescribed snacks is considered a valuable activity in promoting nutritional intake. Touching the resident promotes tactile stimulation; putting an herb plant to a resident's nose increases olfactory stimulation. Playing music reduces resident anxiety and promotes a comfortable environment.

TAILORED ACTIVITIES THAT MEET PHYSIOLOGICAL NEEDS *PROMOTE*

- **Nutritional Intake**
- **Sensory Stimulation**
- **Comfortable Environment**

Addressing the physiological needs of a resident who is in a coma or a semi-comatose state is a difficult challenge since responses to activity services are usually not evident. "Semi-comatose" in this context refers to a resident who does not recognize or communicate with people and does not show any obvious understanding of the environment. An end stage Alzheimer's patient would be an example. Using Maslow's physiological need to view these residents supplies a framework for a philosophical approach to care planning. Each resident's history determines the specific approaches.

Activity services for the comatose and semi-comatose should reflect a 24-hour-a-day strategy involving all the individuals who have contact with the resident. The activity professional is the person who designs the plan, but it requires the support of staff, family, and volunteers. Knowing the resident's background and understanding the resident's physiological need level directs the approaches.

For example, Ms. Luther has severe dementia and does not communicate or feed herself and shows no signs of being aware of her environment other than crying out if she is moved. Ms. Luther took great pride in her eight children and several grandchildren and enjoyed her rose garden. She listened to the news every morning and relished spending time with her several cats. Ms. Luther's activity care plan includes having a radio in her room turned to a news program in the morning. Two or three times weekly, volunteers and her family place a docile cat beside her. They take Ms. Luther's hand and move it along the cat's fur. Her family visit often and talk about her grandchildren. They frequently place roses in her room. The staff and family put the roses close to her nose and rub the soft petals down her cheeks. Everyone who enters Ms. Luther's room is informed of these approaches. Environmental services' staff, nursing staff, volunteers, activity staff, and family members cooperate in implementing these services on an ongoing basis. These approaches make Ms. Luther's environment more comfortable.

Safety Needs

Residents' needs for safety are unmet when their behavior is characterized by a continual expression of fear regarding their environment. A primary option for instilling a sense of security is to structure a familiar daily routine. Activities that are consistent regarding time, place, format, and leader offer reassurance. Any necessary changes are made gradually without increasing the resident's anxiety. Individual activities or small groups are often the most appropriate intervention since the stimulation of a large group can increase a resident's fearfulness. Spontaneous activities, such as sharing a walk with a resident who appears anxious, are frequently as important as planned activities.

TAILORED ACTIVITIES THAT MEET SAFETY NEEDS *PROMOTE*

- **Routine**
- **Reassurance**
- **One-To-One**
- **Small Groups**

Fulfilling safety needs, like physiological needs, is a 24-hour-a-day process involving many people. Constant support by staff, other residents, family and volunteers is necessary to calm a resident who is experiencing severe insecurity. Coordinating the efforts of every person who interacts with the resident begins with a consistent plan of care. When a resident is subjected to capricious approaches, the results can be increased anxiety and even catastrophic reactions, such as combativeness.

For example, Ms. Turpin is a 68-year-old mid-stage Alzheimer's resident who was recently admitted to Unit B of a nursing home. Ms. Turpin worked as a waitress in a restaurant and frequently walks to the Unit B nurses' station asking, "Where is my food order? I have customers waiting, and I must get their food." One evening the nurse at unit B is frustrated because she has answered Ms. Turpin's questions several times. The nurse finally replies to Ms. Turpin in a loud voice, "This is not a kitchen; this is a nurses' station. Don't you see my uniform?" Ms. Turpin looks at the nurse without understanding and goes to the nurses' station on Unit C where she repeats, "Where is my food order? I have customers waiting, . . ." The nurse at unit C replies, "This is not a kitchen, but I will show you where the kitchen is." The nurse then walks Ms. Turpin back to unit B and says, "Here is the kitchen." Ms. Turpin's face shows marked anxiety and she begins to pace rapidly back and forth. Later that evening, she is combative when the staff try to get her into bed. This unfortunate escalation of Ms. Turpin's behavior could have been avoided by using a consistent approach of promoting a sense of security rather than inadvertently producing anxiety.

Reassurance is offered by applying familiar scenarios to the present situation. Ms. Turpin was unable to understand that the nurses' station was not a kitchen. She was much more familiar with a restaurant than a nursing home and tried to apply her past, familiar experience to the current, unfamiliar environment. The following scene is an example of how Ms. Turpin's behavior could have been handled in a different manner. Ms. Turpin goes to the Unit B nurses' station asking, "Where is my food order? I have customers waiting, and I must get their food." The nurse at unit B recognizes her frustration limit with Ms. Turpin's questions and asks a volunteer to take her for a walk around the building. She instructs the volunteer to encourage Ms. Turpin to talk about her waitress job and her family. The nurse also asks the volunteer to stop in the dining room where Ms. Turpin can eat her evening snack. The dietary staff provide a pitcher of lemonade for Ms. Turpin to use to serve drinks to the volunteer and other residents. While in the dining room, a resident volunteer joins

them; she holds Ms. Turpin's hand and reminisces with her. Later that evening, a nursing assistant plays a country and western music tape of Ms. Turpin's choice while helping Ms. Turpin with her ADL care. Ms. Turpin continues to ask many questions about her environment; however, her anxiety is reduced, and no combative behavior occurs. The overall design for this plan is initiated by the activity professional, but its implementation is dependent on a variety of individuals.

Love Needs

Residents perceive themselves as being loved if they have opportunities for positive social interactions either on a one-on-one basis or in groups. Interactions must communicate to the resident that they are accepted without reservation. A more optimal response is obtained when the interactions take place over extended periods of time, at least three months.

> ### TAILORED ACTIVITIES THAT MEET THE NEED FOR LOVE *PROMOTE*
>
> - **Positive Social Interactions Over a Period of Time**

Peer relationships are an important source of comfort to a resident in long-term care since they provide a frame of reference familiar to both parties. Peer in this context refers to someone about the same age. Peers have encountered similar childhood experiences, have lived through the same historical events and often share comparable values and beliefs. If both peers in a relationship live in the facility, the relationship serves as a sounding board regarding the challenges of institutional living. If one peer lives in the community, the resident experiences a connection with the world outside the facility.

Activity programs promote peer relationships through a variety of techniques. Asking residents to introduce themselves at the beginning of a group activity, communicating resident accomplishments through announcements, introducing two residents with a similar interest, rewarding residents for volunteer services, and offering roles to residents, such as mail delivery and program planning, exemplify how to shape peer opportunities.

Community involvement is another avenue for fulfilling residents' needs for positive social interactions. Since society tends to have a negative attitude toward long-term care, favorable community interactions depend on education. The activity professional serves as an ambassador to the community by dispelling stereotypes and providing information about the medical and psychosocial aspects of residents' lives. Building community involvement includes implementing programs with other institutions such as schools, day-care centers, businesses, and service organizations. These programs vary from structured oral history classes, art appreciation studies, and performing choirs or bands to simply inviting the community to less formal activities such as covered dish dinners, special entertainment, and parties. Facilitating new relationships with community members is also done by assigning volunteers to visit specific residents. Community involvement cannot be cursory; it must be a vital, regular part of programming.

Many activity professionals share a common frustration during holiday seasons when community members call and request a visit with residents. These requests usually involve one visit for a brief period of time. The author believes that this limited one-on-one visit is at least inadequate and may actually reinforce a resident's feeling of abandonment when the visitor does not return following the holiday season. In coordinating personal visits between the community and residents for a particular nursing home, the author began asking that community members make a three-month commitment to a resident before personal visits were initiated. While some volunteers rejected this expectation, many community members made firm commitments to residents by stating, "I had not realized how many losses nursing home residents have suffered, and I will gladly accept responsibility for routine visits."

Family members are usually a key factor in meeting residents' love needs. Some families experience uncertainty about their relationships with a resident and need education about how to continue to be involved in a positive manner. Activity programs are an opportunity for families to interact with a resident in a familiar routine. This interaction can affirm the continued value of the relationship. For example, a facility has an oral history class. Passing down family traditions and values from one generation to the next is a normal pattern in many families. The oral history program encourages family members to ask specific questions of a resident, write and/or tape the answers, and help compile the information. The data is shared with other residents, staff, and the community.

Relationships between staff members and residents are important to meeting residents' love needs since these relationships take place over a long period, and staff usually spends a significant amount of time with residents. Staff members need education about how to maintain a professional, yet personal relationship with a resident. Activity programs are an avenue for staff to interact with a resident in a setting that emphasizes the adult roles of both parties. For example, Mr. Bowie enjoys classical music. His nursing assistant, Ms. Porter, prefers rock-'n-roll. During a facility talent show, Mr. Bowie plays a classical piece on the piano and Ms. Porter sings a rock-'n-roll song. Afterwards Mr. Bowie teaches Ms. Porter about the opera, and he asks Ms. Porter to teach him about some of her favorite singers.

Self-Esteem Needs

Participation, responsibility, and opportunities for leadership increase self-esteem. Activities that call for active participation and involve the resident in the final result help restore a sense of accomplishment. Resident councils are an example of how an activity's value is enhanced when residents take part in aspects of problem identification as well as problem resolution.

**TAILORED ACTIVITIES THAT MEET
THE NEED FOR SELF-ESTEEM *PROMOTE***

- **Participation**
- **Responsibility**
- **Opportunities for Leadership**

The author worked with a group of residents who complained during a resident council meeting about other residents who were disoriented and who entered their rooms without permission. Initially, the residents suggested that the staff confine these residents to their rooms and "tie them up." The author provided some basic education related to disorientation and the staff's desire to treat all residents as individuals with different abilities and difficulties. Gradually, the residents began to realize that if the staff dealt with disoriented residents in a harsh manner, the same techniques might be used toward any resident. This realization led to a realistic discussion of probable solutions. The resident council evolved from a stagnant organization into a cohesive team capable of tackling problems and creating solutions. They became participants who could affect change rather than powerless victims with no control.

Traditional approaches to caregiving in nursing homes have not always focused on residents' self-esteem needs. As mentioned in Chapter 3, the initial model for nursing home care was based on a medical model emphasizing disease, resident passivity, and professionals' knowledge and responsibility. This model tends to view residents as being perpetually at the physiological and safety need levels. It limits resident potential to fulfill the highest level of human capacity by assuming residents are not capable of attaining more than basic needs due to multiple physical problems.

Recognition of the comprehensive needs of nursing home residents despite physical functioning deficits has gradually led to a wellness or social model approach. The wellness model encompasses many of the approaches applicable to enhancing self-esteem. It emphasizes resident wellness, involvement, and responsibility. While activity programs have stressed this perspective for many years, acknowledgment of the value of this philosophy in the 1987 OBRA legislation has helped maximize self-esteem programming throughout other services, e.g., nursing, dietary, etc.

Self-esteem activities require the support and cooperation of other disciplines. Without a common understanding of self-esteem needs, residents will not have the necessary opportunities to enhance their abilities and self-worth. For example, Mr. Jones, an oriented 78-year-old resident, is a teacher for an oral history class for third grade students. The class meets on Fridays at 2:00 p.m. Mr. Jones feels a sense of self-esteem when he is able to answer the childrens' questions about his past experiences. Mr. Jones needs assistance with dressing and shaving. His nursing assistant, Ms. Williams, perceives him from a medical model viewpoint, i.e., "I know what decisions to make for him," and at the physiological level, i.e., "He needs to be fed, clothed and showered." Ms. Williams usually gives Mr. Jones his shower and shave in the afternoon. When the activity professional reminds her of the oral history class, Ms. Williams replies, "His shower and shave will have to wait until after the class is finished." Mr. Jones refuses to attend the class without being shaved. He feels a loss in self-esteem due to his lack of control over decision making with regard to his ADLs. This loss is further magnified when he misses the activity experience that highlights his self-worth.

Changing to a broader perspective of residents' needs requires a change in staff's viewpoints. While the regulations already require this, it will not become actual practice without a vigilant education program. The activity professional must be an advocate for the full recognition of all resident needs. This necessitates one-on-one education of individual staff as well as participation in formal in-service training. Documenting resident progress, communicating effectively with other disciplines, ongoing training, and emphasizing positive outcomes are all critical approaches to assuring that the self-esteem needs of nursing home residents are recognized and addressed.

Self-Actualization

Once self-esteem is recovered, residents grow toward self-actualization by involving themselves in creative activities that seek positive solutions to their lives' tasks. This is the most highly individualized need of the hierarchy since individuals at this level have a clear experience of self-esteem and do not rely on others to provide a sense of direction. Activity services primary function is to offer multiple opportunities for self-actualization based on residents' requests for meeting this need. Reminiscence and spiritual activities are two examples that frequently reflect residents' desires for fulfilling self-actualization needs.

Reminiscence is an important tool for assisting the elderly to gain a healthy perspective on their lives. Multiple alternatives exist for program development. Intergenerational or peer oral history classes and spontaneous discussions of past experiences during a familiar activity are common approaches. Some residents may want to make a permanent record of their experiences. Others may want to share their thoughts on an informal, but regular basis as a mentor to a college student. The reminiscent services offered depend on specific resident requests and responses.

TAILORED ACTIVITIES THAT MEET THE NEED FOR SELF-ACTUALIZATION *PROMOTE*

- **Resolution of Life Tasks**
- **Reminiscence**
- **Spirituality**

Spiritual activities are designed to put residents in touch with their most sacred commitments. For example, a resident who is a minister can continue to visit the sick and/or offer prayers for church services. While this spiritual context certainly includes religious-based activities, it also encompasses obligations that may not be stated or thought of in a religious vein. A resident who feels responsibility to the environment can be in charge of special gardening activities or raising money for environmental concerns.

Tailoring Programs to Meet Needs

The development of tailored activities begins by recognizing individuals or groups who do not have their needs consistently met through core activities. This could include any individual or group in the facility. Common examples are the oriented, the severely disoriented, and the profoundly deaf and blind. Identification emerges from individual assessments or program monitoring.

Once identified, the activity professional assesses the need of the individual and/or a common need of the targeted group. The goal of a tailored activity is to meet the identified need. Approaches are developed to provide a format for carrying out the activity in ways that are most likely to meet that need. To adequately address residents' needs, the activity's goal and format is carefully matched to the targeted person's or population's interests and abilities.

For example, an activity is designed with the goal of providing high functioning, oriented residents who rarely attend other activities with an opportunity to increase their self-esteem. Once the need is determined, a common activity interest is identified. The residents for this example have an interest in music. A resident choir is chosen as the activity medium. Hour-long rehearsals are held weekly. All choir members are expected to attend rehearsals and stay through the entire session. Residents are given their own music and are asked to bring it to each meeting. The choir's repertoire is chosen by a majority vote of its members. Each piece is rehearsed until it meets the director's expectations.

Residents who are asked to participate in the choir meet specific criteria. These criteria are based on the identified population's abilities and the format of the activity. Residents need to fulfill these criteria in order to successfully participate in this activity:

1. A capacity to stay through a one-hour activity one time weekly
2. An ability and interest in singing
3. Good memory skills
4. Good social skills

These criteria are a reflection of the activity's goal and format. Note that the activity is based on the type of expectations a choir director in the community setting would have. These are realistic expectations for a high functioning group of oriented residents.

Residents who are in the choir are expected to attend rehearsals, bring their music, and choose the repertoire. This provides multiple opportunities for active participation, responsibility, and leadership. As discussed earlier, these criteria lead to an increase in self-esteem; therefore, the activity's format provides ample possibilities for meeting the intended goal.

The following is another example of the development of a tailored activity. It is discovered that a group of residents of varying abilities are socially isolated and feel unloved. An activity is planned for these residents to meet their need for love by participating in an intergenerational program. The children from a local school are invited to visit for thirty minute meetings that take place two times monthly from September until May. As much as possible, the same residents and children participate in each program to encourage positive interactions over a period of time. During each session, the residents and children work on an art project. Each project has been adapted to common resident problems such as poor eyesight, disorientation, and hemiparesis.

The residents who are asked to participate meet the following criteria:

1. A capacity to stay through a thirty minute activity two times monthly
2. An ability to work on simple art projects with assistance
3. An interest in and an ability to interact positively with children

These criteria are again a reflection of the activity's goal and format. These expectations do not exceed the abilities of this diverse group of residents, but they are necessary for successful participation.

This activity's primary focus is positive social interactions between the elderly and the children over a period of time. This interaction can be expected to result in meeting the residents' need for love.

Adapting the Tailored Activity

Individualized adaptation is the most efficacious method for achieving tailored results. This requires a fluid strategy that cultivates competent participation in preferred activity pursuits by conforming to deficits and abilities. Once the need for adjustment to an activity routine is recognized, specific modifications are applied. These center primarily on two areas: changing the overall structure of the group and individual activity services and modifying the environment. Adaptation in its entirety will not be discussed in this book, but basic ideas to consider in adjusting services will be presented.

Adapting the Structure of Group and Individual Services

Activity programs serve a diverse population of elderly and have limited resources, making it imperative that the activity professional recognize and implement modifications into activities without decreasing their therapeutic value. Changes in approaches can be made if they do not affect the tailored activity's goal. It may be feasible to include residents who do not meet all the established criteria or to further adapt approaches to meet individual needs. Exceptions that have a minimal effect on the final outcome are reasonable and may be appropriately introduced.

For example, Ms. Melbeth (Case Example in Chapter 6, page 65) was included in the choir because of her past interest in music. Refer to the previous resident choir example under "Tailoring Programs to Meet Needs." She did not meet the resident choir criteria (number 1 and number 3, page 74) which required an attention span of one hour and good memory skills. She would have become frustrated if she had been expected to stay for the entire rehearsal. She was placed by a resident who offered her reassurance and could easily leave when she became anxious. This caused minimal interruption to the group. After several weeks, Ms. Melbeth's fear regarding the environment was reduced, and she was able to appropriately participate in the final performance.

In this example, the modifications did not change the outcome. If several residents like Ms. Melbeth had been included in the rehearsals, the number of interruptions would have increased and the high functioning, oriented residents might have refused to attend; therefore, the targeted group would not have met the original goal. Adaptations become inappropriate when the targeted population do not meet the intended goal as a result of too many variations in the format.

Privacy in the provision of individual and group activity programs is a key concept in preserving residents' rights. Constant interruptions of activity programs for medications, showers, and family visits can greatly reduce the positive impact. Closing the door to the activity room or a resident's room and placing a "Do not disturb" sign on the door are helpful techniques in attaining privacy. In-services and frequent explanations of the reasons for this privacy increase understanding as well as respect for the importance of activity programs.

Special Needs Programming is an effective tool in maximizing the therapeutic value of tailored activities. Once the activity professional has identified the residents who will benefit from a particular activity, the activity includes only those particular residents. This focuses the activity on a smaller group of residents and their particular needs and interests. The April 1992 interpretive guidelines for nursing homes instruct surveyors to review whether activities are "designed to meet the functioning levels, needs, and interests of different residents" (Department of Health and Human Services, 1992). Special Needs Programming is an avenue for meeting this guideline by emphasizing individual needs and differences rather than grouping residents together without regard for personal preferences and characteristics.

Coordination of schedules with staff and family members is crucial to Special Needs Programming and privacy. This helps to assure that the residents for whom a tailored activity is designed are in fact present when the activity occurs and that these residents can participate without interruptions. Chapter 8 illustrates a form that facilitates communication regarding scheduling. Special Needs Programming and protection of privacy during activities is easily explained to other disciplines by acknowledging the corollary to providing medicines, therapies, and ADL care according to each individual's situation.

Using tailored group activities rather than individual services is an important adaptation to consider. Human beings are social beings and need frequent opportunities to be in group settings. Tailored group activities often fulfill individual needs that cannot be met through less structured group activities or individual services.

The author works with a resident who has multiple physical problems and is rarely out of his room or bed. For six months, he received individual music therapy services two times weekly. His responses varied from singing-a-long to sleeping throughout the sessions. Recently the nursing staff began getting him up on a regular basis in a recliner. He is taken to a small group music therapy program two times weekly. During this activity, he continues to receive one-on-one attention, but he also has an opportunity to socialize with other residents in a new, stimulating environment. His responses are much more animated and consistent. He observes and speaks to other residents, sings with every song, and never sleeps during the group activity. Individualizing group programs provides part of the solution to achieving effective time management as well as therapeutic programming.

Tailored individual activities are a primary consideration for residents who are unable to benefit from regular group activity attendance and/or who impede the ability of others to participate. For example, Ms. Sawyer is a 71-year-old dementia resident who yells out the name "Bill" constantly. When taken to group activities, her yelling increases in frequency and volume. This disturbs the other residents, many of whom leave the activity. Ms. Sawyer appears to receive no benefit from the group and in fact shows an increase in anxiety. Even during one-on-one conversations in her brightly lit room, she usually yells "Bill", indicating no awareness of another person. The activity professional, Ms. Hartman, begins implementing individual services. These include limiting anxiety producing stimulation while providing a soothing atmosphere. The door to Ms. Sawyer's room is partially closed, the lights are dimmed; and her music preference of jazz is played softly. Ms. Sawyer's yelling decreases, and she speaks on a one-on-one basis to visitors and staff, giving two or three word responses.

Activity length usually varies from a few minutes to one hour. Resident responses direct how long an activity continues. Individual activities, especially for residents with short attention spans, are often more effective when they occur frequently for short periods of time. Activity equipment such as tape recorders, radios, craft supplies, or reading materials should be available in a resident's room so they can be used throughout the day for the length of time comfortable to the individual.

An hour is usually the maximum amount of time a group activity is productive. People who attend meetings on a regular basis can attest to the fact that a group tends to lose its focus after an hour with no break. This same principle is applied to group activities.

Residents who are physically able may desire participation for longer periods of time. The activity professional can facilitate this by providing additional supplies and minimal supervision. For example Ms. Henry is a moderately confused resident who has few physical problems. After an hour-long intergenerational program of stringing cranberries and popcorn, Ms. Henry stays in the activity room, continuing the activity without assistance. The activity professional gives her an ample supply of cranberries, popcorn and string and she occasionally observes Ms. Henry to assure that she is not becoming tired.

A common adaptation is to shorten the length of group activities for residents with low physical endurance or distress. This may involve modifications such as placing residents where they can easily leave the activity area if they become tired or anxious, grouping residents with the same tolerance in one group that meets for a short period of time, and/or recruiting volunteers who can work with a resident in a group on a one-on-one basis.

Seating arrangements are an important consideration in group activities. Placing residents in a circle where they can see each other enhances a sense of group cohesion. Circular seating provides multiple opportunities for eye contact and verbal stimulation. Exercise programs are an example of how this seating increases resident responses. Residents who are disoriented will have multiple visual cues for what is expected because they have a view of all the members of the group. A resident who has only the use of one side can be placed where he/she can observe how another resident with a similar deficit participates in the exercise program.

Tables are a necessary piece of equipment for some activities such as crafts or gardening, but, when there is no particular reason to use tables, the author has found them to be a barrier to socialization. Residents are more likely to reach out and shake the hand of another resident if a table is not between them. It is also easier for residents to leave a room if they do not have to maneuver around a table.

Some residents have more positive responses to activities if they are placed near the door. Examples are residents with short attention spans, residents who are concerned with incontinence, and residents who are anxious. Placement near the door facilitates an early exit without disrupting the group.

Seating arrangements need to consider social, safety, and ability factors. Placing a resident who is anxious and has limited speech next to a resident who is friendly and willing to learn to communicate despite another's speech deficits can nourish a peer relationship. Some residents have hostile relationships with others. Offering these residents a seat away from each other can be important to safety. Residents who share similar interests or abilities are encouraged to sit close together. For example, residents who participate in a choir are encouraged to arrange their seating according to whether they prefer singing or playing rhythm instruments. Seating arrangements do not need to be rigid but can be an important adaptation depending on residents' needs.

Scheduling has a major impact on outcomes. Some residents may respond better to morning activities while others may prefer afternoons or evenings. Reactions to group and individual services are monitored to assess if there is a time of day when a resident's participation is heightened. Services then are scheduled according to the best response period. For example, a facility's dietary department notes that a group of low body weight residents eat better at breakfast since they are more alert and hungry. The activity professional determines that social responses also might be better at this time. An early breakfast for this group of residents is scheduled for the activity room two times a week. It is found that the residents socialize more during this time than any other.

Staff, residents, and community members are excellent resources for adapting activities. Many adaptations require one-on-one supervision. The professional activity staff needs assistance to provide this in a comprehensive manner. For example, nursing assistants and environmental services staff are trained to provide services to residents during their routines of providing care or cleaning rooms. These services usually require a small time commitment. Some examples include placing headphones on a resident and playing a tape, tuning a resident's television to the resident's preferred channel, turning off a television at a time when the resident is not listening, handing a resident activity supplies (e.g., books, a plant to water, and craft projects), and talking to a resident about their activity interests. Residents benefit from activity opportunities throughout their waking hours. This is only accomplished with the cooperation of the entire nursing home staff.

Residents adapt activities by offering peer support, participating in planning, and providing information. The primary peer support most residents experience comes from other residents. This is a useful tool in promoting positive responses within group and individual activities. For example, Ms. Edney is an oriented 76-year-old resident who assists with a small reminiscence group for disoriented residents. Ms. Edney has been a community volunteer with disabled people for much of her life and has a gentle, adult peer approach with the disoriented residents. She is asked to sit next to a resident who becomes anxious. With Ms. Edney holding her hand and prompting responses, the anxious resident stays for thirty minutes of the activity and participates fully. Ms. Edney also is receiving benefits from this participation. In the past few months, Ms. Edney's eyesight has gradually deteriorated. She had lost all interest in activities because she could no longer see to read or participate in crafts. She does not need good eyesight to assist a disoriented resident to participate in reminiscence.

Resident participation in planning and providing information identifies necessary adaptations. Residents understand from personal experience what types of variations are needed and can provide suggestions to each other and to the staff. For example, one facility had a problem with wheelchair traffic jams. Residents identified the problem and participated in resolving the concern. The residents' suggestions included educating other residents about the need to be

courteous in passing other residents in the hallways. A Courtesy Awareness Week was planned to promote education as well as ventilation of feelings. Staff participated by keeping equipment on one side of the hall and removing equipment during peek rush hours. Resident input is a critical aspect for adaptations.

Community volunteers modify activities by offering one-on-one services and expanding the variety of group activity opportunities. Individual activity services include visitation, transportation, reading, playing music, assisting with handwork projects, writing letters, and sharing common interests. Volunteers assist residents during group activities by providing one-on-one assistance that enhances resident abilities. For example, some residents have the physical abilities to play table shuffleboard but lack the cognitive abilities to begin the game. A volunteer helps position the residents at the table and reminds them how to play. The residents then proceed to play successfully with a few occasional prompts from the volunteer.

Community members increase the variety of activity opportunities because of their individual interests and because of the other people they know in the community. For example, a community member, Ms. Connor, brought her baby to the nursing facility to visit the residents. During her visits, she met a resident who was interested in having more contacts with the Jewish community. Ms. Connor was Jewish herself and volunteered to take the resident to her home for meals one time weekly. She also introduced him to other members of her synagogue.

Analyzing the specific steps that make up a given activity facilitates a design for successful participation. Any activity performance involves steps proceeding from one to another in a particular order. For example, participants in an adult day-care center are asked to label newsletters for a local Alzheimer's association. One participant of the center, Mr. Jacobs, has moderate dementia and is unable to place the labels on the newsletters without assistance. The activity professional, Ms. Hartman, analyzes the steps involved as follows. The first step is to remove one label from the label sheet. The second step is to stick the center of the label onto the label area of the newsletter. The third step involves rubbing the three inch label into place. The fourth step requires placing the completed newsletter in a pile. After the four steps are completed, the process starts over again. Mr. Jacobs is unable to complete the four steps without constant supervision. This constant prompting irritates him, and he leaves the activity area. Ms. Hartman discovers, through analysis of the activity and observation of Mr. Jacob's abilities and deficits, that he can complete steps number one and number two without prompting. Ms. Hartman works beside him, completing steps three and four herself. With this approach, Mr. Jacobs is able to complete a task successfully. When all the newsletters are finished, Mr. Jacobs smiles and remains in the room to enjoy refreshments with the other participants.

Adaptive equipment is beneficial for creating optimal activity experiences. Though it is a growing business, adaptive equipment that meets the activity pursuit needs of older impaired adults is relatively unavailable. Most equipment is designed for activities of daily living needs or the recreational needs of younger adults and children. Some adaptive equipment is advertised as being designed for older adults, but the colors and products are similar to children's toys.

Thus, the activity professional often needs to design equipment using facility and community resources. An example of equipment that can be readily built by the facility staff is an adaptive garden. Many resources are available with specific designs. The author has found *Growing with Gardening, A Twelve-Month Guide for Therapy, Recreation, & Education* (Bibby Moore, 1989) and *Horticulture Therapy for Nursing Homes, Senior Centers, and Retirement Living* (Rothert and Daubert,

1981) to be useful in adapting garden projects. Another example is asking an artist to design large print, simple tin punch patterns since most patterns are too complicated or too tiny for disoriented and/or visually impaired residents. Occupational therapists are an additional resource to tap regarding adaptive equipment.

Other equipment is found in catalogues or local stores. Clamps can be used to hold craft projects for a resident who has the use of only one hand. Grips for pens or crochet hooks are helpful tools for residents who suffer from arthritis. Paper with heavy lines and large gaps between lines is purchased or designed for residents with visual impairments to facilitate writing. Talking books are used by residents who are unable to read. Various types of magnifying glasses and hearing enhancement devices also are available. Large print reading material is accessible in libraries and bookstores. This is just a small listing of adaptive equipment. The activity professional needs to research catalogues for specific equipment to meet individual resident needs.

Physical and verbal prompting is perhaps the most important adaptive approach. Physical prompting occurs when a person takes a resident's hand or arm and demonstrates how the resident is to complete, for example, an exercise. It also can occur when a person demonstrates, with his/her own actions, how to complete an activity task or touches a resident to show approval or support of a resident's efforts. Verbal prompting refers to verbal instructions or words of encouragement. Prompting must be done in a manner that encourages participation, while not defeating a resident's sense of independence. If a resident receives too much physical or verbal prompting, he/she becomes overwhelmed with a sense of dependency. A resident's response is usually obvious from facial expressions and actions or lack of actions. Many of the adaptations already described have included some form of physical or verbal prompting.

Adapting the Environment

An assessment of how the environment positively affects the activity experience involves an evaluation of the facility's physical structure and other services. The facility's physical structure refers primarily to the activity space. Activity space refers to any area where an activity can take place. This space may include residents' rooms, dining areas, designated activity rooms, hallways, and offices. Space considerations relate to when the space can be used, how many spaces there are, where it is located, the size of the space, the storage space available, and the atmosphere. The more activity spaces available on a regular basis, the more flexible and pervasive the activity program becomes. For example, Mr. Jones is an oriented resident of a nursing home who refuses to participate in activity programs. He spends his day staring at a wall across from his room, never speaking to anyone. One day, the activity professional posts a crossword puzzle on this wall. Gradually, the staff and visitors begin stopping at the crossword puzzle and filling in the answers. One day, a staff member is expressing frustration over not finding one of the answers when Mr. Jones says, " 'Hiccup', the answer is 'hiccup.' "

Location and size of the activity room frequently are reasons for adaptation. Some activity rooms are located in remote areas of the building, requiring the use of an elevator, and/or taking long periods of time for transporting. One adaptation may be having small group activities in areas such as lounges that are closer to resident rooms. If the activity room is too small to accommodate a large group activity, the dining room may be used for some activities. Some adaptations may affect other important aspects of activity approaches such as privacy. If the dining room is used for activities, staff and residents who are not participating need to be informed

of when the activities are taking place so there will not be a constant flow of disruptive traffic.

Storage space becomes an issue when activities are held in areas not designed for activity use. Adaptations include carrying equipment on carts or scheduling activities that require a lot of equipment in a space with adequate storage. Storage space might be made available in nearby offices or by building shelves in a lounge or dining area.

Atmosphere has a positive or negative affect on resident participation. Colors, pictures, designs, noise, or objects are a few factors influencing the atmosphere. Colors, pictures, and designs should be carefully studied when a room is being planned or remodeled. Environmental design is a growing field, though much is still not known about how certain colors, designs, etc., impact human behavior. The effect often depends on individual preferences and specific deficits. For example, red is more easily seen by many older adults but may agitate a resident with dementia. Ultimately, adaptations are a compromise of what suits the majority of residents' needs the best. Public announcement systems that constantly interrupt activities can agitate residents and decrease participation. A possible adaptation is to have a switch placed on the system so it can be shut off during activities. Disoriented residents may find windows that face a parking lot distracting. Closing curtains or changing rooms are possible approaches to consider.

Evaluating how other services interface with the activity program is important to adapting the environment. The activity professional should have a thorough knowledge of the goals and approaches of other services in the facility. This is obtained through care plan and staff meetings, reading, and one-on-one interactions. Integrating services is an important adaptive device. For example, a facility offers a "Step Up Exercise" Program using the resources of the activity and restorative nursing departments. The restorative aide leads a small group exercise program for severely physically debilitated clients. After residents gain more physical endurance, they are discharged from the restorative program to an exercise program for moderately impaired residents led by the activity department. Combining efforts assures residents have ongoing opportunities for exercise that meets their physical needs.

Adaptation can involve a significant amount of time to assess the resident and the activity and then to apply the adaptation. It is important to consider the amount of time saved when residents have positive rather than negative outcomes. In the example of Mr. Jacobs and the task analysis of the newsletter labeling, the activity professional spent one-on-one time with him. This appears to be a large investment. However, when Mr. Jacobs is not involved in meaningful activity pursuits, he becomes agitated, belligerent and sometimes combative. This behavior often requires two or more staff members' time. Another consideration is the fact that once the activity professional has done an evaluation of the adaptations necessary, they can be used by volunteers or support activity and nursing staff members.

SUPPORTIVE, MAINTENANCE, AND EMPOWERMENT OUTCOMES

Core activities provide a program foundation that addresses general functioning problems, and Maslow's Hierarchy gives a framework for developing a tailored program to meet specific needs. Designing core and tailored activities directs the program toward positive outcomes. Supportive, maintenance, and empowerment activity experiences are indicators that these outcomes actually have occurred. These three experiences are the essential consequence of cultivating opportunities that foster a satisfying activity pursuit pattern for individual residents.

The April 1992 federal interpretive guidelines for nursing facilities require an activity program to be "multi-faceted and reflect each individual resident's needs." This program should provide "stimulation or solace, promote physical, cognitive and/or emotional health, enhance to the extent practicable each resident's physical and mental status, and promote each resident's self-respect by providing, for example, activities that allow for self-expression, personal responsibility and choice" (Department of Health and Human Services, 1992). Supportive, maintenance, and empowerment activity experiences were described in Chapter 2 as they apply to the entire spectrum of human endeavors. Here the discussion will center on how to use these concepts to recognize desirable outcomes for individual residents and to adapt approaches if the expected outcomes are not occurring.

Activity attendance is sometimes used as a gauge for positive resident outcomes. Simple attendance can be used as a valid measurement for assessing part of the overall amount of activity involvement. It is not, however, an indication of the activity's relevance to a resident's life. A resident may attend activities, but not relate to other people in the activity or recognize or manipulate the activity space. Attendance may happen without participation. Involving oneself in choices and individualism is not reflected in simply being present. Outcome indicators go beyond cursory observations to reveal a resident's actual experiences.

Supportive, maintenance, and empowerment results are recognized by discovering the response an activity inspires. This text will present some common indicators of these experiences as a reference point. They are mere guidelines. Each resident's personal situation persists as the ultimate criteria.

Supportive Activity Experiences

Residents who have supportive activity experiences feel a sense of belonging. This belonging includes relationships with other people and the environment. Optimally, relationships with people encompass family members, other residents, staff members, and the community. Interaction with the environment comprises at least the long-term care facility and when possible, the community outside.

Some of the items on the MDS reflect a resident's sense of belonging. MDS Section III—Customary Routine (Appendix A-1, page 116) reveals some of the resident's relationships prior to admission. For example, "Moves independently indoors" (f.) shows a resident's interaction with his/her previous environment. "Daily contact with relatives/close friends" (q.), "Usually attends church, temple, synagogue, etc." (r.), and "Involved in group activities" (u.) refer to relationships with other people. MDS Section B—Cognitive Patterns (Appendix A-2, page 117) has several pertinent items. A resident's knowledge of "Location of own room" (3b.), "Staff names/faces" (3c.), and "That he/she is in a nursing home" (3d.) affect the ability to negotiate the current situation. A resident who has a "Changing awareness of (the) environment" (5b.) encounters frustration and even terror. Review the other sections of the MDS for indicators of a resident's interactions with people and the facility's surroundings.

The Activity Therapy Assessment is a resource for determining whether supportive activity results are present. Refer to the assessment form in Chapter 6, pages 36-37, 39-40 (Figure 6.1a-e) for the following example. Ms. Smith's history shows she sang professionally all her life. However, though she performed with a group of people, her assessment indicates that she currently has no desire for group participation. This limits her supportive activity experiences. She does have a relationship with a nursing assistant and they sing together. This is an initial step in Ms. Smith's comfort level. Yet she refuses to propel her wheelchair, limiting her sense of belonging to her environment. These initial findings form the strategy for increasing supportive outcomes.

Once a resident has an opportunity to interact with the activity program, indicators of supportive activity experiences begin to emerge. These include a concern for establishing a specific activity routine and a desire to control activities. A resident's desire to create an activity routine is expressed verbally and nonverbally. A resident may specifically state, "I want to attend this activity again." Residents may request that their ADL care not conflict with their activity pursuit schedule. A resident in one nursing facility refused to take physical therapy in the afternoon because it interfered with her participation in a volleyball game. Thereafter, the physical therapist arranged to provide therapy in the morning. Residents may routinely place themselves in the same location in an activity, e.g., by a specific window or door and/or may always sit by the same person.

SUPPORTIVE OUTCOME INDICATORS

- **Concern for Establishing an Activity Routine**
- **Desire to Control Activities**

Establishing an activity routine can be expected of the majority of residents, including the moderately demented and sometimes even the severely demented. A confused resident may consistently and without assistance find and stay in a location where a pleasant activity has occurred. In one facility where the author worked, the activity staff frequently involved a confused resident in conversations even though her speech was rarely coherent. This was done primarily by imitating the emotions she expressed, e.g., when she laughed, the activity staff laughed, when she cried, the staff spoke empathetically. This activity usually happened at the door of the activity office. After a few weeks of this approach, the resident began to independently find the activity office and spend her day in conversations with passersby.

People who feel like they have a relationship with their environment are comfortable enough to try to manipulate it. This is why residents who take control of a given aspect of an activity are indicating they feel a sense of belonging. For example, the activity professional, Ms. Frost, was helping Ms. Melbeth (case example from Chapter 6, page 65) transplant a geranium into a larger pot. Ms. Frost decided that the geranium was successfully planted and began putting the supplies away. Ms. Melbeth took more potting soil from the bag and began to add it to the pot. She then asked Ms. Frost where the watering can was located. Ms. Melbeth felt comfortable enough to take control of the activity, establishing her own ability to manipulate part of her environment. Whether a person lives in a long-term care setting or in the community, a sense of belonging can be exemplified by establishing an activity routine and taking control of specific aspects of an activity pursuit pattern.

Residents who do not indicate a sense of belonging merit further evaluation and changes in their plan of care. Lack of response is never automatically considered an expected part of a resident's condition. Instead poor results or no response is an opportunity for deeper exploration. This is true even for residents who may be unable to indicate their experiences of activities such as the semi-comatose or comatose. The following example is based on an actual case.

Mr. Randolph is a 76-year-old end stage Alzheimer's resident. He shows no signs of recognizing staff or family members and is unable to interact with the environment. He receives complete assistance with his care. His activity assessment shows he frequently listened to country and western and bluegrass music prior to the onset of his current condition. The activity care plan approach is to take Mr. Randolph to all group music programs. After six months, he exhibits no response.

The activity professional, Mr. West, knows Mr. Randolph might be unable to make a recognizable response to music due to his semi-comatose state. He also believes a review of the resident's preferences and current situation might reveal other approaches that could be more effective in promoting a sense of belonging. The nursing staff report that Mr. Randolph responds to auditory sensory stimulation such as loud noises in his room. In speaking to Mr. Randolph's son about his father's relationship to the environment, it is found that Mr. Randolph often remarked "There is nothing like a good rain to make you feel the power of nature."

The care plan is changed as follows: country and western and bluegrass music and environmental sounds of rain are played via headphones regularly. Headphones are used because they bring the sound closer to Mr. Randolph's environment, his body. During the country and western music tape, Mr. Randolph's feet begin to move to the beat of the music. When the rain tape is played, Mr. Randolph looks up as if expecting to feel wet drops. This example shows that careful consideration of a resident's sense of belonging can identify more

personalized services. It is possible, with a resident like Mr. Randolph, that no response would have been noticed. Nonetheless, using specific music and environmental tapes with headphones is far more individualized to his situation than taking him to every group music program.

A sense of belonging for residents who are mostly unresponsive is dependent on caregivers recognizing them as individuals. A resident who is unable to communicate a distinct identity is at risk for being treated as a body rather than a human being. The approaches implemented for Mr. Randolph illustrated his individuality. His humanity and his right to be treated differently from any other resident were validated. The ability of the activity care plan to illuminate the value of human beings augments the supportive experience.

Maintenance Activity Experiences

Residents who have maintenance activity experiences attain optimal health. Optimal refers to the maximum health possible given the residents' deficits. All areas of functioning, i.e., physical, cognitive, social, and emotional, are relevant to maintaining fitness. Participation is an inherent aspect of maintenance outcomes because health benefits do not result from passivity.

The MDS is an initial reference point for establishing maintenance activity outcomes because it offers a perspective regarding a resident's potential participation abilities and records areas that require activity interventions. For example, in MDS Section E—Physical Functioning and Structural Problems (Appendix A-3, Item E, page 119), shows the amount of assistance a resident needs with eating. If a resident is shown to eat independently, but does not participate in activity pursuits that are comparable with regard to skill level, e.g., gross motor crafts and exercises, the resident is probably not participating at the maximal level.

Residents who have unsettled relationships (MDS Section G, Appendix A-3, page120) or behavioral or mood problems (MDS Section H, Appendix A-3, page 121) are candidates for aggressive activity interventions. These interventions involve cultivating resident participation in activities that build social skills and encourage positive emotional expression.

The activity assessment form has several questions relating to a resident's past and current maintenance activity participation. Under "Activity Pursuits & Related Abilities" (Chapter 6, Figure 6.1b, page 37), every item has information relevant to the desire to participate, actual participation or the ability to participate. This data holds clues for developing a plan that encompasses each aspect of functioning and facilitates maximum involvement.

A resident's activity pursuit pattern with regard to participation in activities that promote physical, cognitive, social, and emotional functioning demonstrates the results of maintenance activity experiences. Physical activity participation involves any activity where the resident exerts physical energy. An exercise class is one example. There are many other activity pursuits that require physical exertion but may not be viewed as such. Singing is not usually thought of as exercise, and yet it provides an excellent format for developing lung capacity. Gardening and crafts require fine and gross motor movements. Walking or propelling a wheelchair to an activity necessitates physical effort and should be credited as a maintenance result.

MAINTENANCE OUTCOME INDICATORS
PARTICIPATION IN ACTIVITIES
THAT *PROMOTE*

- **Physical**
- **Cognitive**
- **Social**
- **Emotional Functioning**

Maximizing physical activity requires interdisciplinary coordination of programs that mutually promote participation in activity pursuits and activities of daily living. Each resident's optimal level of physical endurance is determined and then team members develop a plan to match physical needs with services. For example, when a resident is discharged from physical therapy, the interdisciplinary care plan team coordinates an exercise plan addressing the resident's needs and abilities. A restorative aide is assigned to walk the resident, and a nursing assistant is designated to encourage range of motion exercises. The activity professional reviews the assessment and finds interests that can be used in promoting physical activity. A resident who has an interest in gardening is involved in daily gardening projects. If the resident needs to increase upper extremity strength, the resident is encouraged to hold a hose and water the outdoor garden and transplant large plants. If the resident needs to improve fine motor skills, caring for seedlings or making dried flower arrangements are viable approaches.

Optimal participation requires knowledge of physical limitations. The activity professional is aware of the physical endurance level to assure that participation does not exceed safe levels. Trigger number 4 of the Activities RAP (Appendix B) is concerned with a resident becoming physically distressed due to overexertion. The activity professional can use the physician's order discussed in Chapter 6, page 44 and information from restorative and rehabilitative services staff to assess physical capacity.

Cognitive activity participation includes any activity where the resident uses thinking skills. The level of participation is dependent on the resident's maximum ability. Thinking abilities include expression of thoughts, completion of an activity task, and/or attention to an activity. Expression of thoughts is done verbally or nonverbally. One resident participates in a discussion of current events by sharing lengthy information about a topic, while another resident participates by shaking or nodding his/

her head in response to questions. Completion of an activity task involves an entire project or one step. An oriented resident completes a craft project independently, while a moderately demented resident finishes one step. Attention means focusing on an activity for a period of time. One resident stays through a one hour gardening activity, while another resident sits just long enough to plant a few seeds.

Social outcomes include participation in any activity where socialization occurs. Positive relationships with family, staff, volunteers, and other residents promote social functioning. Interactions are verbal or nonverbal. A resident may initiate social contacts by seeking out others with a handshake or waving. Verbal conversations occur in a variety of locations, e.g., during telephone calls, activity programs, eating in a dining area or going down a hallway. Dementia does not limit a resident from having social contacts. The author has frequently watched two cognitively impaired residents have lengthy conversations. While the content of the verbal language was not clear, the residents' body language, i.e., smiles, frowns, voice intonations and gestures, were indicative of communication. Some residents cannot initiate conversations, but they respond when coaxed. This behavior also constitutes positive social interaction.

Emotional outcomes are exemplified by the expression of all types of feelings. This includes verbal and nonverbal expressions. A resident gives verbal feedback to the staff during a Resident Council meeting regarding the facility's services. Another resident smiles and laughs during an activity. Nonaggressive expressions of anger are positive outcomes. Expressions of anger imply that a person feels strongly about something and believes, that by expressing this, it will be acknowledged and necessary action will be explored. When a resident cries during the singing of a favorite song, it is a healthy expression of feeling. However, if crying persists and becomes routine, it merits further exploration.

Developing an activity care plan which promotes health involves assuring that the resident has a balanced activity pursuit pattern. Participation in all of the functioning areas is necessary to achieving optimal maintenance outcomes. For example, Ms. Marietta James is a resident who engages in cognitive and psychosocial activity pursuits, but she rarely participates in physical activity. The activity professional educates Ms. James about the importance of all types of participation. One possible approach might be to include more physical exercise in the activities she already attends. Ms. James enjoys a reminiscing class where various topics, e.g., music, recipes and dating rituals, are discussed, but no physical activity occurs. The activity professional could add some physical exercise relevant to the activity's theme, e.g., dancing to music from Ms. Jame's childhood, picking food from a garden, and making recipes or playing old fashioned games such as croquet.

Empowerment Activity Experiences

Residents who have empowerment activity experiences possess a sense of control over their lives. They search for a variety of options regarding activity pursuits and take responsibility for expanding preferences. The ability to seek and make choices is a primary outcome.

The MDS furnishes data about resident choices. Section G—Psychosocial Well-being (Appendix A-3, page 120) identifies whether the resident "Pursues involvement in life of facility (and) responds positively to new activities . . ." General Activity Preferences, in Section I—Activity Pursuit Patterns (Appendix A-4, page 121), list resident selections with regard to activity setting, general activity preferences, and preferences for more or different activities.

The activity assessment form is used to determine past and current desires to make choices. Reviewing the number of activity preferences as well as the number of options a resident explores within a specific activity illustrates a resident's ability to access a variety of alternatives. The question "Group & Individual Activities Resident States He/She Will Participate In" (Figure 6.1b, Part 2, page 37) helps gauge a resident's current desire to explore possibilities. For example, a resident who is interested in empowering experiences is curious about the types of activity services the facility and community offer. He/she seeks some type of leadership role such as planning the activities. This resident takes an active role in determining his/her activity pursuit pattern.

Empowerment outcomes are identified by assessing whether the resident experiences enriched, self-designed choices. These choices are made individually and with others in groups. The resident initiates discussion of preferences and does not rely on others for prompting. Seeking leadership roles in designing specific group activities or serving on problem-solving task forces reveal a desire to impact decisions. Searching for new activity choices or new ways to approach an activity are common pursuits.

> ## EMPOWERMENT OUTCOME INDICATORS
>
> - **Enriched, Self-Designed Choices**

Empowerment outcomes usually take a longer time to occur than supportive or maintenance outcomes. A number of factors affect this evolution. A resident's sense of dependency upon entering the facility may be generalized to all areas of life, e.g., "I can no longer walk independently, therefore, I cannot make independent choices about other aspects of my life." Society tends to have a view of nursing homes as a place for sick people who cannot make choices. Residents are likely to share this perspective, believing that living in an institution is synonymous with having no control. This happens even when a facility uses a wellness or social model.

Cultivating empowerment experiences during the first assessment interview inspires a resident's confidence about decision making. During the first contact, the activity professional makes the resident aware of the choices available on the formal activity schedule, the accommodations that can be made to this schedule to match the resident's needs and individual services that will be tailored to the resident's preferences. It is crucial to demonstrate in the first few weeks that honoring choices is a sincere commitment.

Mr. Craig has enjoyed classical music all his adult life. He has a specific interest in pipe organ music and his favorite composer is Bach. Upon his admission to a nursing home, no classical music programs are scheduled. Mr. Craig does not have access to his tape recorder or music tapes due to his wife's illness. The activity professional, Ms. Frost, loans a tape recorder to Mr. Craig and borrows some Bach organ music tapes from the local library. Ms. Frost also consults Mr. Craig regarding the scheduling of classical music programs for the next month. Mr. Craig volunteers to call some local music teachers and ask for their assistance. Ms. Frost's timely follow-up in adapting the individual services and activity schedule to Mr. Craig's preferences gives him an increased sense of control over his situation. This sense of control is illustrated by his taking responsibility to contact the music teachers.

The variety and level of choices depends on residents' desires and abilities. Maximizing each person's autonomy is accomplished by adapting services to enhance all realms of decision making. Resident involvement in planning and implementing activities with minimal or no guidance from the staff is at one end of the spectrum. Reducing extensive verbal and physical prompting as residents gain competence is at the other end. One severely demented female resident enjoyed listening to music via headphones and a tape player. Initially the staff placed the headphones on her head and turned on the tape player. After several weeks, the staff continued to turn the music on, but the resident placed the headphones on her head and removed them without assistance. This was one of the only choices she was able to independently accomplish. The value of having some control, however limited, is of absolute importance to well-being.

Residents are especially cautious about making choices within a group until they are comfortable with the group's leader, purpose, and members. This wariness is a normal aspect of group dynamics in or out of the institutional setting. Empowering activity outcomes in groups require careful cultivation of residents' confidence through dynamic leadership and facilitation skills.

The activity professional facilitates groups with a sense of clear direction while creating adaptations to enhance individual results. The amount of leadership provided depends on the group's requirements. Residents need to be familiar with the expectations of the group. These expectations initially are identified by the leader with input from group members. Resident input is usually tentative at this point. As the activity professional becomes familiar with the group's participants and residents become familiar with each other, individuals' strengths and interests are used to increase resident-driven choices. For example, a member of the gardening group who is an expert on flowers is asked to give advice regarding the care of the rose garden. Once the member's advice is heeded, this individual is likely to initiate recommendations without prompting. Other group members observe this and gain confidence in the safety of expressing preferences.

The group leader fosters an atmosphere of respect among the members. This means that each member's choices are given equal merit. The leader does not allow residents who speak more forcefully to override the preferences of other group participants. When residents are secure in the knowledge that their opinions and those of others will be honored, they grow in their ability to seek autonomy within the group. As residents' confidence in the group increases, the activity professional's role changes as it requires less direct involvement.

Group empowerment experiences are evident when a group explores a variety of activity options and assumes responsibility for making decisions. Much of the empowering experience takes place by having and acting on choices related to project completion. Examples of project goals are art shows, music performances, or craft displays. Preferences about how, where, and when an activity is carried out comprise many of the valuable choices residents pursue. For example, a group of residents meet to plan a Christmas play. The activity professional serves as a group facilitator by providing information related to budget and scheduling information, when other Christmas events are planned, and what day and time families have indicated as a preference. The activity professional also helps residents learn to communicate with each other. One resident, Mr. Jones, uses a computer-generated voice. The activity professional asks Mr. Jones to demonstrate how the computer works. The other residents learn to wait until Mr. Jones types his answers and pushes the voice button.

The play's theme, who should play what role, specific date and time and costumes are decisions the residents determine. They discuss a variety of options related to each area. When the discussion is completed, the theme is established, the roles are assigned, and the date and time are set. The residents request that the activity staff check into the cost of renting choir robes. Planning this event is an empowering experience.

Summary

Supportive, maintenance, and empowerment outcomes provide a useful framework for examining whether activity programs are positively impacting resident lives. They provide a basis for documenting results in individual medical charts, a reference point for developing quality assurance studies, a tool for survey agencies to determine expected outcomes, and an instrument for measuring the impact of activity programs on the well-being of nursing home residents. The next chapter will explore how to integrate assessment information, program planning, quality assurance studies, and outcome measurements into a documentation system that works to improve the quality of life for nursing home residents.

9 INTEGRATION

The final step in building a results-oriented activity program is the integration of resident assessments and programs with outcome measurements. This includes the use of a coherent documentation method that promotes the design and implementation of activity care plans and the ongoing monitoring of the program's effects. Establishing this process is one of the most critical aspects of realizing optimal resident outcomes.

Documentation Method

This section encompasses a discussion of documentation concepts and a presentation of a method using specific forms. Recording activity services and residents' responses is required by regulations and standards of practice. These requirements serve as guidelines. The primary force directing documentation is resident outcomes.

Many health care professionals consider paperwork to be burdensome because it often is perceived as taking time away from resident care. When documentation flows from a framework that engenders maximal resident benefits, it becomes a tool of care, not a diversion from care. This means developing assessments, implementing care plans, and providing services for the sole purpose of achieving optimal resident participation in preferred activity pursuits. The concepts and forms introduced in this chapter have been used satisfactorily in accomplishing this result. The reader is encouraged to take the materials presented here and creatively use them in ways that will foster resident well-being.

The documentation method includes the following forms: an initial assessment, a problem list, a care plan, a service record, a progress note, and a communication tool. All of these forms are placed on the medical chart except for the Activity Therapy Service Record (Figure 9.4, page 98) and the Activity Therapy Resident Attendance Schedule (Figure 9.7, page 105). The service record is a daily monitoring method on which the periodic documentation is based. It should be considered a medical record even though it does not need to be placed in residents' charts. The attendance schedule is a communication tool that helps augment resident involvement in activities.

Specific forms are not required to complete any of this documentation. If a narrative format is used for problem lists, care plans, progress notes, or activity therapy service records, it is important to follow an outline as was discussed with activity therapy assessments. This outline can be developed using the criteria set forth on the forms presented here. The attendance record also can be done using a variety of methods. The reader should consider the purposes that these tools serve and not the specific forms, as the primary directive for developing a manageable documentation system unique to his/her own job situation.

Figure 9.1 (page 92) demonstrates the flow of the documentation placed on the medical chart. This method provides a developmental picture of the resident's interaction with the activity program from the time of admission until discharge. This system makes readily available pertinent information for evaluating and improving activity services.

There are multiple interrelationships between the forms introduced in this chapter and the MDS. Some examples will refer to two or more forms. For this reason, the reader may want to copy all of the forms or mark the pages they appear on for easy and quick reference.

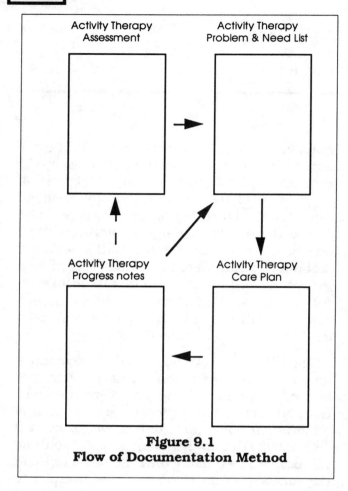

| Activity Therapy Assessment | Activity Therapy Problem & Need List |
| Activity Therapy Progress notes | Activity Therapy Care Plan |

Figure 9.1
Flow of Documentation Method

affect this awareness: responses to activity involvement and changes in functioning. When a resident reacts positively to activity pursuits, he/she moves up the hierarchy. When a resident's activity participation is stagnant or decreases, the same need continues or a regression to lower levels results. Subtle or extensive deterioration or improvement in a resident's functioning or new problems affect perceptions of the current situation, and consequently, individual needs.

Most residents have essentially the same general problems throughout their stay in a facility, though the symptoms and behaviors may change dramatically. Identifying general problems rather than detailed behaviors or symptoms on the problem and need list is helpful in focusing the care plan's attention on cultivating innovative approaches rather than describing the specificity of problems. Behaviors and symptoms are more appropriately recorded in progress notes and assessments. New problems are added to the form when variations in a resident's physical, cognitive, social, or emotional status create changes that are not already listed. When a problem is resolved or there are no feasible activity approaches, it is inactivated.

The Activity Therapy Problem and Need List

The Activity Therapy Problem and Need List (Figure 9.2) is an organizational tool facilitating consistent numbering of the same problems and needs throughout the resident's stay in a facility. This list identifies only those areas related to therapeutic activity programming and is initially constructed from the weaknesses recorded on the resident's assessment. Compare Figure 9.2 to the weaknesses shown on Ms. Smith's assessment in Chapter 6, (Figure 6.1e, page 40).

Residents' current needs are reflected on this list. Maslow's Hierarchy again is used as a framework. These needs depend on each individual's changing or constant perception of his/her circumstances. Two primary influences

The Activity Therapy Care Plan

The activity therapy care plan pinpoints problems, approaches, and goals that are specific to the situation of each resident. The initial assessment and periodic progress notes provide detailed information about residents' problems and needs, current and past lifestyle, and responses to activity pursuits and/or activity services. This is the foundation on which the activity therapy care plan is built.

Routine time intervals for writing activity care plans are primarily dependent on the requirements of the state and federal regulations, facility policies, and practice standards. Periodic reviews are generally completed every two to three months. The discovery of additional resident preferences, resident's responses to activity services, or significant changes in a

Figure 9.2
Activity Therapy Problem and Need List

NAME _Jane Smith_   ID# _xyz_

Date	Prob. / Need #	Problem	Date Inactivated
10/19/92	1	Feels Unloved/Needs Attention	
10/19/92	2	Decreased Mobility	
10/19/92	3	Poor Communication Skills	
10/19/92	4	Limited Current Involvement in Activity Pursuits	

resident's status may merit more frequent reviews of the activity care plan and/or require substantial changes in the plan.

The initial care plan is written following the completion of the initial assessment. This is usually within one to two weeks after admission. Forming a relationship conducive to attaining specific preferences and a distinct, personal understanding of a resident's problems and needs in a one or two week period is unrealistic. Some facility policies and state regulations require a one month review after the initial care plan is completed. Considering the number of losses a resident is dealing with during the initial stay, such a review policy is worth considering.

The activity therapy care plan is reviewed immediately and may require substantial modification if a resident's status changes significantly. Alterations are only necessary if the resident's change in status affects the activity care plan. There may be instances where a change in a resident's medical status requires only the review of the nursing care plan, not the activity care plan. For example, a resident needs a change in medications due to a urinary tract infection. If this infection does not limit his/her current level of activity participation, the activity professional does not need to change the care plan. In the example of Ms. Smith's (Chapter 6, page 63) sudden onset of blindness, it was imperative that her activity care plan be updated immediately and several new approaches implemented. If Ms. Smith's care plan had not been changed quickly, the potential for substantial deterioration in both her needs and problems would have been significant.

Activity care plans yield a more complete understanding of each resident's preferences and responses to activity services as the length of stay in a facility increases. In the case of Mr. Fredrick (Case Study, Chapter 6, page 64), his care plan became more specific over a longer period of time and more effective in addressing his individual situation.

Integrating activity therapy care plans with interdisciplinary care plans is an important factor to consider in designing documentation systems. There are two primary methods for achieving this integration. One method incorporates all care plans onto one form. This technique is effective if it provides the necessary detail required and all disciplines' problems, goals, and approaches are interrelated and not just consecutively listed.

The other method focuses on putting all common interdisciplinary problems, goals, and approaches on one form while listing discipline-specific plans on another. This method is useful in streamlining the interdisciplinary plan without losing the integrity of the activity care plan. The author has a personal preference for the latter, but ultimately resident outcomes determine the appropriate choice for a given facility. The documentation system presented here assumes that activity care plans are written in detail on one form and relevant aspects of the plan are incorporated into the interdisciplinary plan on another form.

Resident involvement in the plan of care is necessary to success. Asking the resident for input increases the resident's control over personal choices as well as provides the activity professional with relevant information. Chapter 3 discussed specific approaches for enhancing resident participation. The Activity Therapy Care Plan form (Figure 9.3, page 96) has space for recording comments a resident has expressed regarding the plan.

Contacting family and significant others routinely (and only with the resident's permission) when the care plan is reviewed communicates the value of the activity services the resident receives and helps identify any barriers to these services. This input also affords an opportunity to gain family and community support in increasing a resident's activity pursuit involvement. If a resident is nonresponsive and unable to participate in the care plan, a family member's input can be used in designing the approaches.

Problems

The Activity Therapy Care Plan form (Figure 9.3) is the third step in the documentation method. Chapter 6 gave a detailed description of how to identify problems and needs. Under Primary Problems/Needs (Figure 9.3), the current weaknesses are copied from the Problem and Need list (Figure 9.2, page 93). The related approaches and goals use the same numbers. Goals and approaches regarding Ms. Smith's need for love (number 1) will always be referred to as number 1. Consistency in numbering presents a clear picture of the resident's current and past problems and needs and the coinciding activity approaches and goals.

Approaches

Previous chapters have given numerous examples of how to identify approaches through assessment. In addition, the Resident Assessment Protocol for Activities (Appendix B, page 125) suggests additional areas to explore for evaluating why a resident does not have an optimal activity pursuit pattern. Once these avenues have been probed, approaches are developed from the findings.

Activity services are designed according to the assessment of each resident's activity pursuit pattern. This includes examining the level of activity participation, individual and/or group activity preferences, type of activity preferences, and the personal meaning of activity pursuits (Refer to Chapter 6's discussion of Activity Pursuit Patterns as well as supportive, maintenance, and empowerment outcomes (Chapter 8). Refer to Ms. Smith's care plan (Figure 9.3). Ms. Smith's assessment (6.1a-e, pages 36-37, 39-40) and initial MDS (Figure 4.2, page 25) reveal that she spends little time in activity involvement. All of the care plan approaches are aimed at increasing her overall level of participation. To address Ms. Smith's need for love, approaches are implemented to reflect her valued relationship with Deanna (individual relationship preference), her interest in gospel music (specific activity preference) her interest in a group setting (group preference), and her pride in her singing abilities (meaning of activity pursuit).

Supportive, maintenance and empowerment approaches also are apparent in the care plan. The 10/19/92 approaches to Problem number 1 (Figure 9.3) support the relationship between Ms. Smith and Deanna. This relationship is likely to give Ms. Smith a sense of belonging. Approaches Update to Problem number 3 on 11/19/92 with regard to teaching Ms. Smith to operate the tape recorder encourage her to manipulate her environment. Both plans for Problems number 2 and number 3 promote participation in exercise and communication. These are maintenance related activity approaches. The plan for Problem number 4 on 10/19/92 fosters increased activity choices, an avenue to empowerment.

Activity Therapy Goals

Activity therapy goals reflect each individual's potential interaction with the activity program. Goals, like approaches, employ information about the resident's activity pursuit pattern. This information is transformed into terms that describe frequency, activity media, and specific behaviors. These criteria provide an objective measurement that is suitable for documentation purposes. Frequency is determined by the resident's choice, the resident's physical endurance level, and how often the activity is offered. Activity media are developed from the resident's activity pursuit preferences. Specific behaviors are based on expected supportive, maintenance, or empowerment outcomes. Ms. Smith's goal number 1 on 10/19/92 (Figure 9.3) which states that "Resident will participate in gospel sing-a-long 1 time weekly" identifies the frequency ("1 time weekly"), the activity medium ("gospel sing-a-long"), and the maintenance behavior ("participate").

Chapter 8 described the results of supportive, maintenance and empowerment experiences. The goals that follow in the next paragraph are examples of how to relate these experiences to measurable goals. The examples

Figure 9.3
Activity Therapy Care Plan

NAME *Jane Smith* RM # *101* ID # *xyz*

Date Initiated *10/19/93* Date Reviewed *11/19/93*

PRIMARY PROBLEMS / NEEDS
1. Feels Unloved/Needs Attention
2. Decreased Mobility
3. Poor Communication Skills
4. Limited Current Involvement in Activity
   Pursuits

PROBLEMS / NEEDS UPDATE
1. Continue
2. Continue
3. Continue
4. Continue

APPROACHES
For Problem (1)
(a.) Ask nursing assistant, Deanna, to accompany resident to gospel sing-a-longs; (b.) Compliment resident's singing; (c.) Introduce her to others

For Problem (2)
(a.) Place on Tone-Up Club List & invite 3 x weekly; (b.) Compliment her participation in exercises; (c.) Provide 1 to 1 instructions as needed

For Problem (3)
(a.) Ask yes/no questions & wait for response; (b.) Ask family to bring tape recorder & tapes of her choice; (c.) Encourage singing for self-expression

For Problem (4)
(a.) Visit one to two times weekly to establish rapport & expand activity pursuit involvement; (b.) Gradually increase participation by offering frequent & varied choices

APPROACHES UPDATE
For Problem (1)
Continue a, b & c; Add (d.) Activity staff to invite her to music programs, e.g., gospel sing-a-longs & entertainment

For Problem (2)
Continue a, b & c; Add (d.) Remind nursing staff to check Tone-Up Club List & have resident ready for activity; (e.) Instruct in wheelchair mobility to & from activity

For Problem (3)
Continue a & c; Add (d.) Teach resident to operate tape recorder

For Problem (4)
Discontinue a.; Continue b.; Add (c.) Invite & take resident to garden class (d.) Ask family to place geranium in her room

GOALS
For Problem (1)
Resident will participate in gospel sing-a-long 1 x weekly. (1 month)

For Problem (2)
Resident will participate in Tone-Up Club 1 x weekly. (1 month)

For Problem (3)
Resident will sing with taped music of her choice 2 x monthly. (1 month)

For Problem (4)
Resident will identify one additional activity preference. (1 month)

GOALS UPDATE
For Problem (1)
Goal Met, New Goal: Resident will participate in gospel sing-a-longs with Activity Staff 1 x weekly and attend entertainment programs 2 x monthly. (3 months)

For Problem (2)
Goal Not Met, Continue (3 months)

For Problem (3)
Goal Met, New Goal: Resident will learn to operate tape recorder independently. (3 months)

For Problem (4)
Goal Met, New Goal: Resident will participate in group garden projects 2 x weekly & care for a plant in her room. (3 months)

This Was Reviewed (X) Was Not Reviewed ( )
With Resident
Resident indicated she is hesitant about attending groups but she would attend with Deanna.

This Was Reviewed (X) Was Not Reviewed ( )
With Resident
She agreed to attend Tone-Up, garden activities & gospel sing-a-long & learn to use the tape recorder.

SIGNATURE *Karen Frost, ACC* SIGNATURE *Karen Frost, ACC* do not list specific activity media since they depend on resident preferences nor is frequency indicated since it can vary dramatically. Ms. Smith's activity care plan can be reviewed to understand how activity media and frequency are used.

The outcome of supportive activities is a sense of belonging. The following are some related goals: resident will form peer relationships; resident will establish a specific activity routine; and resident will show a desire to manipulate all or part of an activity. For the semi-comatose or comatose resident who is unable to participate, the following are examples; resident will receive visits from family and friends; and resident will have a familiar activity routine provided by staff, volunteers, and family members.

The expected result of maintenance experiences is participation. Sample goals could be: resident will participate in a physical activity; resident will interact with another person; resident will share information; and resident will express an opinion.

Empowerment outcomes give the resident a sense of control. Written goals might include: Resident will make choices regarding activity preferences; resident will participate in planning activities; and resident will increase his/her activity choices.

The Activity Therapy Service Record

Objective goals are based on a measurable system of documentation. This documentation must be specific with regard to time frames and content. It needs to record frequency, specific activity media, resident responses and reasons for nonattendance. For example, a resident's goal is to participate in art class three times weekly. To measure this goal, a system is developed to document the frequency of attendance to art class and whether participation occurs. If attendance does not occur, the system should identify the reason.

Refer to the Activity Therapy Service Record in Figure 9.4 (page 98). Using this form, it is possible to document the frequency of attendance to specific activities and the response as well as reasons for lack of attendance. A master list of abbreviations for specific activities, behaviors, and causes for nonattendance should be established and made accessible when the service record is filled out. The bottom of this form shows a sampling of abbreviations that apply to Ms. Smith. If other activities, behaviors, or reasons for nonattendance need to be tracked for a specific resident, but are not on the master list, abbreviations can be added to this form under Comments and/or Pertinent Observations.

Tracking attendance to specific activities helps identify what approaches produce the best results. As has been discussed, specific activity preferences are more pertinent to resident responses than general activity categories. For example, a resident attends a small group exercise class led by an aerobics teacher and also attends a large group where residents exercise to a videotape. Both activities use the same general activity medium-exercise. The resident participates in the small group class but falls asleep in the large group. Obviously, the small group produces a better response. The service record should be able to distinguish the small group exercise class from the large one. This record contains valuable information for facilitating optimal exercise for this resident.

Recording behaviors shows whether the results desired have been achieved. Supportive, maintenance, and empowerment outcomes are verified. Review the resident behaviors at the bottom of the Activity Therapy Service Record (Figure 9.4). Staying in an activity denotes comfort level. Participation and socialization show maintenance of functioning. Making choices relates to empowerment. Figure 9.4 demonstrates that Ms. Smith participates in gospel singing activities but not in Tone-Up Club. She attended a party but did not socialize. The 11/19/92 progress note (Figure 9.5) records these behaviors and the 11/19/92 care plan

Figure 9.4
Activity Therapy Service Record

Name: Ms. Jane Smith   Month: October   Year: 1992   Room #: 101

Activity	1	2	3	4	5	6	7	8	9	10	11	12	13	14	15	16	17	18	19	20	21	22	23	24	25	26	27	28	29	30	31
Politics																															
Cards/Other Games																															
Crafts/Arts						AT R																									
Exercise/Sports					TC R		TC (P-)		TC A	TC A	TC R	TC A	TC A				TC A	TC A	TC R	TC A				TC R	TC R	TC A	TC R				
Music (Gospel is Preference)							GS (P+)							GS (P+)							GS (P+)							GS (P+)			
Reading																															
Writing																															
Trips/Shopping																															
Walking/Wheeling Outdoors																															
Watching TV																															
Intergenerational																															
Pets																															
Gardening													GD R																		
Cooking																				CO R											
Religious/Spiritual																															
Other/Specify Party														(So-)																	

COMMENTS AND/OR PERTINENT OBSERVATIONS

SPECIFIC ACTIVITY ABBREVIATIONS: TC = Tone-Up Club; AT = Small Group Art Therapy; GS = Gospel Singing; GD = Gardener's Delight; CO = Cooking Class

INDICATE RESPONSE WHEN ATTENDS AND CIRCLE:
RESIDENT BEHAVIORS = S+, Stayed; S-, Did not stay; P+, Participated; P-, Did not participate;
So+, Socialized; So-, Did not socialize; C+, Expressed a choice; C-, Did not express a choice

INDICATE WHEN INVITED AND DOES NOT ATTEND:
REASONS FOR NONATTENDANCE: R, Refused;
A, ADLs not complete; Sl, Sick; V, Visitors

(Figure 9.3) is changed to facilitate better participation, comfort level, and increased decision making.

The reason a resident does not attend an activity is equally important when evaluating the goal and designing new approaches. Common reasons for nonattendance include lack of invitations to attend, illness, schedule conflicts, ADL care not complete, refusal to attend when invited, and visitors. Inviting residents to activities is a critical approach to enhancing resident involvement and should be recorded. Every time a resident is invited to an activity and does not attend, the reason is documented on the service record. This documentation verifies if lack of invitations is a barrier or if other reasons for nonattendance exist. If a system documents why a goal is not met, it is possible to adapt the care plan accordingly.

The service record is similar to a nursing flow sheet and should be used in a like manner. Daily documentation of attendance and responses is important to an accurate record. Filling out this form can be done in a short period of time. For example, in a 120 bed facility, it takes fifteen to thirty minutes to document on every resident's activity participation. This record is primarily designed to document involvement in group activities. Individual activity services for residents who are active in group activities also can be documented on the Activity Therapy Service Record (Figure 9.4).

This form is inadequate for documenting individual activity services for residents who attend few or no group activities and/or who participate in few independent activity pursuits. These residents require routine, detailed documentation since they need frequent one-on-one services. The quality of these services is tracked to assure that they are effective. Individual activity service records should identify the resident's problems and needs, the related goals, the specific activities to be used, the frequency of service delivery, and the resident's responses.

Activity professionals should design a form that encompasses all these areas. This form is used by activity personnel, volunteers, and others who provide the actual service. For example, individual approaches for a resident who needs increased stimulation includes playing taped classical music via headphones. The goal is: "Will respond to music tape by moving rhythmically to the music." The individual service record accommodates documentation of the goal as well as the resident's responses and the specific approaches used. Since one music tape may elicit a more positive response than other tapes, the specific tape played is indicated. This documentation is completed immediately following each visit. When the care plan is reviewed, the activity professional has concise information for framing the next care plan.

The Activity Therapy Progress Note

The activity professional should set aside a block of uninterrupted time to complete the progress note. This time is considered an individual resident service. It is an opportunity to interview the resident about lifestyle choices, activity preferences, and satisfaction with activity services. Completing the progress note also includes interviewing family and staff, reviewing related records, writing the progress note, and updating the care plan accordingly. When this process is given respect, it becomes valuable time spent serving the resident.

Most of the preparation for the progress note is completed just prior to the interdisciplinary care plan meeting. This preparation provides the activity professional with the necessary information to present a succinct, comprehensive picture of the resident's current situation to the team. The meeting also yields additional information that is incorporated into the actual writing of the progress note and care plan update.

The activity therapy progress note is a periodic reassessment of the resident's current functioning and needs. It also identifies the resident's response to the activity therapy care plan, the activity services that have been provided, and additional resident preferences. The Activity Therapy Progress Note form (Figure 9.5) consists of four main areas: Functioning and Needs, Group Activity Participation, Responses and Services, Individual and Independent Activity Participation, Responses and Services, and More or Different Activity Preferences/Choices. It is recommended that the reader review this form, observing its overall design and then read the specific content.

Information about the resident's current functioning and need status helps establish whether the previously identified weaknesses are resolved. A descriptive narrative of specific behaviors, symptoms and responses supplies objective documentation about a resident's current situation. Refer to Current Physical/Emotional/Social Status & Needs and Current Level of Orientation under Functioning and Needs (Figure 9.5a). These sections verify whether functioning problems and needs continue and their scope.

For example, Ms. Smith's progress note states that she "continues to be dependent in mobility" (Current Physical/Emotional/Social Status and Needs). It does not stop at this general statement, but gives an explanation, i.e., "She has refused to learn to propel her wheelchair independently. She continues to be dependent on staff for tasks she can accomplish and demands frequent attention." This additional description indicates Ms. Smith's decreased mobility is due in part to her refusal to propel her wheelchair and is not solely related to a physical limitation. It shows that her need for attention and dependency on others compounds her mobility deficit. This is vital to understanding the nature of her problems and needs and designing relevant solutions.

Other areas of the form also furnish related data about the status of problems and needs. Descriptions of group, individual, and independent activity participation and responses identify the resident's activity pursuit pattern. The General Listing Of Groups Attended & Frequency (Figure 9.5a) summarizes the types of groups attended and verifies how often the resident is involved. This illustrates resident choices and is an indicator of changes in preferences over time. This category and Average Group Attendance Per Month are measurement tools for noting increases or decreases in participation. Compare the progress note with the service record (Figure 9.4) to ascertain how the daily tracking of activity participation is translated to this periodic documentation. Individual & Independent Activities & Frequency (Figure 9.5b) tracks preferences and participation routines related to nongroup activities. Data from these sections of the progress note can be combined with other factors about time spent in receiving treatments (e.g., medications, ADLs, etc.) to determine the overall activity pursuit time involvement pattern.

An additional tool that can be used in conjunction with the progress note is MDS Section I. This provides a standardized format for showing activity time involvement, changes in activity setting preferences, general activity preferences, and more or different choices. Refer to Ms. Smith's MDS Section I (Figure 9.6). This is an update of her initial MDS. It was completed simultaneously with her 11/19/92 progress note (Figure 9.5).

Compare Figure 9.6 with the initial MDS Section I found in Chapter 4 (Figure 4.2, page 25). This comparison validates continued weaknesses and illustrates improvements. Her activity involvement continues to be recorded as "little" (Figure 9.6). This was determined from the details supplied by the progress note. This verifies that Limited Current Involvement in Activity Pursuits, number 4 of the Activity Therapy Care Plan (Figure 9.3), is still a need. Ms. Smith's progress is evident in two areas. Her preferred activity settings now include her own room *and* the day/activity room. Her general activity preferences have increased from three preferences to four. MDS Section I provides

Figure 9.5a
Activity Therapy Progress Note

NAME _Jane Smith_ (fictitious name)   ROOM # _101_   ID# _xyz_

FUNCTIONING AND NEEDS

Current Physical/Emotional/Social Status & Needs

Resident continues to be dependent in mobility. She has refused to learn to propel her wheelchair independently. She continues to be dependent on staff for tasks she can accomplish and demands frequent attention, for ex., she does not attempt to assist in her ADLs, and rings her call bell, often with no specific request. She rarely initiates social contacts with her peers, but she is attending a few activities. She does continue to become frustrated when she cannot express herself verbally.

Current Level Of Orientation

Continues to be unable to state situation, time, place, and person verbally, but gestures and yes/no responses indicate she is oriented x 4.

Intervention Techniques Used For Disorientation and/or Memory Loss & Response

NA

AT Endurance Level _1_   Diet _Regular_

Precautions _None noted_

Rehab Therapies _NA_

Mode Of Transportation To Activities _Wheelchair with Total Assistance_

Special Treatments _None_

GROUP ACTIVITY PARTICIPATION, RESPONSES, AND SERVICES

General Listing Of Groups Attended and Frequency

Gospel Sing-a-long (1 x weekly), Tone-Up Club (1 x monthly), Special Events (1 x monthly)

Average Group Attendance Per Month _6_

Response to Group Activities & Adaptations/Services

Resident was accompanied to the gospel sing-a-longs by Deanna, nursing assistant. Activity staff complimented resident's singing. She was initially hesitant about attending and participating; however, verbal reassurance from Deanna and activity staff assisted her and she now regularly participates. She was placed on the Tone-Up Club attendance list 4 x weekly and invited to attend. She attended 1 x monthly, refusing to participate. She refused to attend about 1 x weekly and was receiving her ADL care about 3 x weekly during Tone-Up Club. When introduced to others during activities, she smiled and extended her hand. She did not initiate any contacts with her peers. Activity staff have used yes/no questions and waited for her answers with good results. She was invited to other activities, but she refused to attend.

Figure 9.5b
Activity Therapy Progress Note

Name   Jane Smith (fictitious name) _____   **ID#** ____ xyz ____

INDIVIDUAL & INDEPENDENT ACTIVITY PARTICIPATION, RESPONSES, AND SERVICES

General Listing of Individual & Independent Activities & Frequency

Resident listened to taped music (gospel & jazz) 2 to 4 x weekly. She had visits from her family 1 x weekly. She listened to her radio daily. She received mail about 2 to 3 x weekly. The community choir director visited occasionally.

Response to Individual & Independent Activities & Adaptations/Services

- ❑ **Large Print Material**   ☒ **Mail is Read Per Resident's Request**
- ❑ **Headphones**   ❑ **Communication Enhancement Device**

At the request of the Activity Staff, the resident's daughter, Ms. Hamlin, brought a tape recorder and tapes of resident's choice. Family members played tapes for resident during their visits. Activity Staff have informed family of resident's participation in sing-a-longs, and they have complimented her on this participation. Resident also has been visited by the Activity Staff and volunteers 2 x monthly to encourage her to sing with tapes. She has responded to these visits by singing along with tapes. Activity Staff asked resident if she would like to learn to operate a tape recorder and she answered "Yes".

MORE OR DIFFERENT ACTIVITY PREFERENCES/CHOICES

Activity Staff have visited resident 2 x weekly to assess new interests, and she has indicated she would like to participate in group and individual garden projects.

Other Notes

As per interdisciplinary care plan, activity staff kept resident's feet elevated during activities.

Signature _____ *Karen Frost, ACC* _____   **Date** 11/19/92 a generalized glimpse of resident improvement, stability or deterioration in activity pursuit patterns.

Response to Group Activities and Adaptations/Services and Response to Individual & Independent Activities & Adaptations/Services (Figure 9.5) record reactions to specific activity experiences and approaches. Group attendance and frequency as discussed previously provide a basis for determining aspects of a resident's activity involvement. These are, however, cursory measurements of activity pursuit patterns.

Resident's actual responses to activities and the activity care plan are the central factors for determining therapeutic value.

Documenting a resident's responses includes negative and positive responses as well as no response. Varied reactions furnish a framework for making comparisons and for better understanding a resident's preferences. A resident may have a more favorable response because of a particular activity media used, the group leader, the time of day, the others who attend, or many other reasons. These factors are verified in the progress note and foster a design for successful results.

Figure 9.6
Section I. Activity Pursuit Patterns: Ms. Smith's 11/19/92 Progress Review

1.	TIME AWAKE	(*Check appropriate time periods* over last 7 days) Resident awake all or most of time (i.e., naps no more than one hour per time period) in the:	
		Morning a. ✓ Evening	c. ✓
		Afternoon b. ✓ NONE OF ABOVE d.	
2.	AVERAGE TIME INVOLVED IN ACTIVITIES	0. Most--More than 2/3 of time 2. Little--less than 1/3 of time 1. Some--1/3 to 2/3 of time 3. None	2
3.	PREFERRED ACTIVITY SETTINGS	(*Check all settings* in which activities are preferred) Own room a. ✓ Outside facility d. Day/activity room b. ✓ NONE OF ABOVE e. Inside NH/off unit c.	
4.	GENERAL ACTIVITIE PREFERENCES (adapted to resident's current abilities)	(*Check all PREFERENCES* whether or not activity is currently available to resident) Cards/other games a. Spiritual/religious activities f. ✓ Crafts/arts b. Trips/shopping g. Exercise/sports c. ✓ Walking/wheeling outdoors h. Music d. ✓ Watch TV i. ✓ Read/write e. NONE OF ABOVE j.	
5.	PREFERS MORE OR DIFFERENT ACTIVITIES	Resident expresses/indicates preference for other activities/choices 0. No 1. Yes	1

Documenting the frequency of adaptations and services is a valuable consideration in evaluating results. Ms. Smith's goal of participating in Tone-Up Club (goal #3) was not met (Figure 9.3). The number of times she was invited to this activity could be a determining factor in her attendance. The progress note documents that she was invited four times weekly (Figure 9.5a). This information is verified on the Activity Therapy Service Record (Figure 9.4). This shows that the approach of inviting her to the exercise program was adequate to obtain the desired result. Other areas are probed to understand why the goal was not met.

The progress note points out problems in service delivery. This facilitates making changes that assure the care plan regimen is efficacious. Ms. Smith's progress note reveals that her ADL care was not completed when she was invited to Tone-Up Club (Figure 9.5a). This happened three times weekly. Refer again to the Activity Therapy Service Record to confirm this data (Figure 9.4). This merits further exploration. For example, is Ms. Smith refusing to get out of bed in time to receive her ADL care prior to Tone-Up Club or is her nursing assistant not aware of the need to accommodate Ms. Smith's activity choice to attend the exercise program? In reviewing Ms. Smith's care regimen, the latter is found to be the case. Refer to the Activity Therapy Care Plan (Figure 9.3) 11/19/92, Approaches under number 2. The activity staff begin reminding the nursing staff about Ms. Smith's exercise schedule and the need to have her care provided prior to the program.

The progress note may not always provide sufficient data to determine a change in care delivery. When this is the case, further investigation is warranted to discover the root of the problem. This will be discussed later in this Chapter under "Ongoing Monitoring of the Program's Results."

More or Different Activity Preferences/ Choices Requested (Figure 9.5b) is a place for recording details about residents' constantly changing preferences. This lays out new criteria for updating the care plan. It also facilitates a discussion between the activity professional and the resident about new interests and plans for the future.

Communicating the Activity Plan to Other Staff

The activity care plan cannot be adequately evaluated unless all aspects of the plan are carried out. A clear, consistent system of written communication enhances the probability of follow through. All disciplines who are involved directly or indirectly in the approaches are notified of their involvement. Physical therapy schedules may need rearranging to accommodate a resident's attendance to a specific activity. Nursing assistants may need to get a resident out of bed and dressed at a certain time. A communication system provides a heightened awareness of the individual activity care plan to all staff. If the system is written it will remain consistent regardless of staff turnover or assignment changes.

One of the most important tools of communication is an attendance list. Each attendance list identifies the place and time of a specific activity and who is to attend (Figure 9.7). These lists are updated as changes occur. An attendance list is used to increase communication with volunteers, other activity staff members, and other disciplines. When the activity plan is initiated, the resident is placed on the appropriate list according to his/her preferences. Specific approaches are listed as needed in the comment section. The lists then are distributed to the relevant sources.

This list helps in coordination of scheduling, but it also serves as a transportation guide. Getting residents to the activity of their choice at the right time and in the right place is one of the greatest challenges to effective activity programming. The attendance list is used by all the people involved in transporting residents.

Figure 9.7
Activity Therapy Resident Attendance Schedule

ACTIVITY NAME Tone Up Club   **Day** Monday

Date 11/19/92

LOCATION Activity Room   **Time** 10:30 am

ROOM #		RESIDENT NAME	SPECIAL NOTE
100			
101	A	Ms. Smith	
	B		
102	A		
	B	Mr. Fredrick	
103	A		
	B		
104	A		
	B		
105	A	Ms. Jones	
	B		
106	A		
	B		
107	A		
	B		
108	A	Ms. Kimble	
	B		
109	A		
	B		
110	A		
	B		

ROOM #		RESIDENT NAME	SPECIAL NOTE
117	A	Ms. Edgewood	
	B		
118	A	Mr. Norton	Needs recliner
	B		
119	A		
	B		

The activity professional needs to be aware of residents' responses to those activities that the activity staff does not provide. For example, many churches provide religious services and other types of activities on weekends and evenings. The activity staff are not always in the facility during these events and therefore are not able to observe who attends or responds positively or negatively. When volunteers or nonactivity staff members are in charge of activity programs, they use this attendance list to indicate who attended and their responses and who did not attend and why. The author has had success in getting volunteers and other staff to use this form effectively.

Ongoing Monitoring of the Program's Results

Ongoing monitoring of activity services produces an objective measurement for assuring that therapeutic activities are integrated with resident assessments and lead to positive outcomes. This quality assurance process gauges the activity program's success and/or nonsuccess in enhancing activity pursuit patterns. Discovery of the reasons for positive or negative results is essential to maintaining the program's benefits and eliminating its failures. Two strategies are of particular value. One is tracking individuals' progress, and the other is routine monitoring of overall program trends.

Tracking Individual Progress

Completion of assessments, care plans, and progress notes is one example of following individual progress. The Activity Therapy Progress Note (Figure 9.5) is designed to stimulate the activity professional to evaluate the effectiveness of the services provided while completing the form. For example, the activity professional, Ms. Frost, reviews the progress note of Ms. Hanes. Ms. Hanes' activity service record indicates that she has not attended any group activities since admission. She has been invited to various activities including exercise class, entertainment, and pet therapy about two to three times weekly, but she has refused to attend any of these programs. Through observation and discussion with other team members, Ms. Frost notes that Ms. Hanes is becoming increasingly withdrawn and seldom goes out of her room. She spends most of her day staring out the window and expresses no enjoyment of solitary activities.

In reviewing the initial assessment information, Ms. Frost notes Ms. Hanes expressed an interest in gardening. She is not listed on the Activity Therapy Resident Attendance Schedule list for Garden Club and has never been invited. Ms. Frost expresses concern to Ms. Hanes about her lack of participation, noting her refusal to attend group activities and her lack of in-room hobbies. Ms. Frost asks if she would agree to attend the Garden Club at least one time monthly over the next three months and if she would take care of a plant in her room. Ms. Hanes agrees. Ms. Frost places her name on the Garden Club list and instructs the activity and nursing staff to consult this schedule routinely. She accompanies Ms. Hanes to the activity room where Ms. Hanes picks out a plant for her room.

Completion of Ms. Hanes' progress note, resident interview, and activity care plan resulted in a clear strategy for reaching a goal based on the resident's activity pursuit preferences and current needs. Expressing concern for Ms. Hanes and gaining her commitment to participate in gardening helped Ms. Frost develop a favorable plan. Encouraging her to choose a plant to care for initiated one approach immediately. Placing Ms. Hanes on the Garden Club list will serve as a reminder of the plan until the next review. The result is likely to be an increase in Ms. Hanes' socialization and a restoration of her participation in a meaningful activity pursuit. Every time a progress note is written, it is an opportunity to monitor the efficacy of services and make necessary alterations.

Routine Monitoring of Overall Program Trends

Reviewing individual cases does not always furnish adequate information about trends that impact service delivery and outcomes as a whole. Routine monitoring of overall program trends is necessary to gaining a comprehensive perspective. Trends refer to a routine set of circumstances that involve a number of variables within the activity department or pertain to the activity department's interface with other services and the community. Detailed information about these circumstances is necessary to understanding how the program functions and how and when the design needs changing. The documentation system presented previously is a valuable tool for attaining this data.

Methods for tracking program trends vary according to the result desired. Two types will be discussed here. One method collects general, often cursory, program data. This method serves diverse purposes including providing material for management reports and staff evaluations and verifying problems in service delivery. The second method matches information about general aspects of the program directly to resident assessments. This method expands the first one into further exploration by identifying whether services are designed to achieve maximum resident outcomes. It is usually more time consuming and involved than the first method. Both methods evaluate trends that affect program results.

Once program trends are verified, the results are used to institute changes to optimize service delivery. Another study is done to establish whether these changes have actually affected the trends. Either of the two methods can be used in a follow-up study. The first method evaluates whether the program modifications have impacted general aspects of the program. The second method is the best one for assessing if program alterations have influenced overall resident outcomes.

Collecting General Program Data

General program data usually refers to the numbers and types of services provided and the numbers of residents attending as well as problems in providing these services. It is helpful in identifying increases or decreases in services, changes in types of services, or road blocks that interfere with the provision of services. This can be used for writing reports to the administrator to show program offerings, general resident responses, areas that need more staff, or community support or equipment needs.

One way to collect data on the number and types of activities scheduled and the number of residents attending is to adapt the Activity Therapy Service Record (Figure 9.4). Replace the resident's name at the top of the form with the words "Group Activity Tracking." After each general activity category, the number of residents attending is listed under the correct date. This form then is routinely completed for every activity each month.

One use for this information is for staff evaluations. The author supervised an activity therapy assistant, Ms. Karen Frost, who had excellent skills in creating activity programs that increased resident attendance and participation. She deserved a significant raise for her efforts. However, the author needed to convince the administrator that Ms. Frost was worthy of more investment. By comparing the number of activities and the number of residents attending prior to Ms. Frost's hire with the results after her three-month employment, it was found that 25 percent more activities were offered per month and resident attendance had increased by 35 percent. This data provided the necessary documentation for convincing the administrator that Ms. Frost should be rewarded for her productivity. Ultimately, the most important factor for evaluating Ms. Frost's work was the difference it made related to resident outcomes, however, for the purpose of obtaining a raise, these statistics were sufficient.

General problems in providing services to individuals are shown on the Activity Therapy Service Record (Figure 9.4). Once recorded, these problems need further assessment to determine the specific cause and significance. They may relate to such areas as resident motivation, scheduling conflicts, lack of communication, or illness. For example, during routine monitoring of the activity service record, it was found that several residents who could benefit from a morning exercise program were frequently receiving their ADL care during this activity. Ms. Hartman, the activity professional, checked to see if the nursing staff had been notified of the benefits these residents could receive from the exercise activity. She discovered these residents were listed on the Activity Therapy Resident Attendance Schedule (Figure 9.7, page 105) at the nurses' station.

Ms. Hartman showed the data on the service record to the nursing supervisor. Since this record was formatted in a similar manner to a flow sheet, the supervisor easily understood the data's credibility. A discussion ensued which revealed several clues regarding the service delivery problem. The residents who were receiving their ADL care during the exercise program were "heavy care residents"; they required a significant amount of nursing staff time, usually due to profound physical functioning problems. The timing of the activity compounded the difficulty. Due to the hectic morning work schedule, i.e., showers, making beds, and physical therapy appointments, the nursing staff found it difficult to have all the residents who needed exercise ready by the morning activity.

Several approaches were implemented using the input of the nursing staff. In addition to the four times weekly morning exercise classes, two more classes were scheduled for the early afternoon. This was planned to accommodate the exercise needs of these particular residents as well as the reality of the nursing schedule. Residents were interviewed to determine preferences for the morning or early afternoon program and ADL care was provided accordingly. After these changes, the attendance and nonattendance of these heavy care residents were monitored through the Activity Therapy Service Record (Figure 9.4, page 98). After a period of three months, the documentation was reviewed to evaluate whether the problem continued. Since it was found that the residents who could benefit from exercise were now attending the exercise class, further intervention was not needed. If these residents had continued to not attend the exercise program, more study would have been required.

Matching General Data to Assessments

Reviewing general aspects of a program such as attendance can result in valuable changes; however, monitoring must go beyond broad findings to more individualized data. The most critical evaluations of activity programs focus on resident outcomes. This requires attention to detailed information about resident needs and preferences. For example, increases in overall resident attendance at activities does not necessarily mean these activities are addressing residents' interests. Many activity programs have large attendances when Bingo is offered. It is often not clear if this is due to the popularity of Bingo or the scarcity of a diverse activity schedule. Resident assessments can determine whether preferences are being considered in service delivery. The following quality assurance example is an actual study done in a nursing home facility. It shows how to relate assessment data to general program aspects and make changes that lead to improved results for individual residents.

Quality Assurance Case Example

The study's goal was to identify group activity programs that were effective and to explore areas for improvement, specifically in serving individual needs. The study consisted of three parts. Part One identified types of residents with regard to physical and cognitive functioning and levels of group activity involvement. Part Two was a calendar audit to determine the types of group activities offered and the skill levels required. Part Three collected data on resident interests. All data collected came from a random sample of fifty residents on two wings in the facility.

Part One

Definitions for physical and cognitive functioning and group activity involvement were used to yield consistent results. High Physical Functioning referred to a resident with no major physical impairments beyond short-term conditions such as a fractured hip. This resident could participate independently in activities. Medium Physical Functioning was a resident with moderate physical impairments such as one-sided paralysis, fair vision and hearing, and fair motor skills. Low Physical Functioning was a resident with severe physical impairments such as blindness, deafness, coma state, severe contractures, extremely low endurance, and/or this resident was in bed most of the time.

High Cognitive Functioning referred to residents with no major cognitive, judgment, or memory impairments who could follow two- or three-step directions and provide some or all of their own activity programming. Medium Cognitive Functioning residents had moderate cognitive, judgment, and memory deficits and could follow one- or two-step directions on their own or with moderate assistance. Low Cognitive Functioning had severe impairment of cognitive, judgment, and memory abilities and required maximum assistance to complete tasks or were unable to complete tasks even with assistance.

Group Involvement included group activity attendance, responses to group activities, and reasons for nonattendance. Group activity attendance referred to the average monthly attendance over the previous three months. Responses to group activities were defined as follows:

1. Participates, no assistance
2. Participates, verbal prompts
3. Participates, hands on assistance
4. Passive

5. Unaware of Activity, Activity Leader or Others in Group
6. Sleeps

Reasons for nonattendance were as follows:

7. Refuses Group
8. In Bed during Group
9. Visitors during Group

Part Two

The second part of the study consisted of a calendar audit to determine the group activity media offered and the level of skills required to successfully participate. The audit recorded all scheduled group activities over the previous three month period. For each of the three months, one Activity Therapy Service Record (Figure 9.4) was used to record the date an activity occurred under the specified category. Any exceptions to these general classifications were listed separately.

In addition to classifying activities by media, each activity was analyzed according to the physical and cognitive abilities required for successful participation. Definitions for skill level paralleled the functioning definitions. Activities designed for multiple skill levels were identified according to each level accommodated. High Physical Activities referred to activities designed for residents with no major physical impairments beyond short-term conditions such as fractured hips and residents who could participate independently. Medium Physical Activities were for residents with moderate physical impairments such as one-sided paralysis, fair vision and hearing, and fair motor skills. Some assistance or adaptations were used. Low Physical Activities were for residents with severe physical impairments such as blindness, deafness, coma state, severe contractures, extremely low endurance, or who were in bed most of the time.

High Cognitive Activities served residents with no major cognitive, judgment, or memory impairments. These activities required residents to follow two- and three-step directions and/or participate independently with minimal supervision. Medium Cognitive Activities were for residents with moderately impaired cognitive, judgment, and memory deficits. These activities required residents to follow one- or two-step directions on their own or with moderate assistance. Low Cognitive Activities were for residents with severe impairment of cognitive, judgment, and memory abilities. These activities provided maximum one-on-one assistance in completion of tasks or did not require any resident participation.

Part Three

The third part of the study focused on resident preferences. This was done by auditing the assessments of the fifty residents in the study for past and current activity pursuit choices. The assessment form presented in Chapter 6 was the routine tool used by the facility for documenting activity assessments. Compare the Activity Therapy Assessment (Figure 6.1b and c) and the Activity Therapy Service Record (Figure 9.4) forms. Notice that they both list the same activity categories. This similarity was helpful in this study for cross referencing information between the calendar audit and the resident assessments. Any additional preferences were recorded individually.

Study Results

This study yielded a vast amount of information. The number of questions the data could answer was nearly limitless. Keeping the original goal in mind, (to identify group activity programs that were effective and to explore areas for improvement, specifically in serving individual needs) the questions were narrowed down to twelve. The following presents the basic findings and illustrates the value of this type of study and the impetus it provided for change.

The study identified the following:

1. The number of High, Medium, and Low Physical Functioning Residents in the sample
2. The number of High, Medium, and Low Cognitive Functioning Residents in the sample
3. The average activity responses of High, Medium and Low Physical Functioning residents
4. The average activity responses of High, Medium, and Low Cognitive Functioning residents
5. The number of activities in the last three months designed so that residents whose functioning was high, medium, and low physical and high, medium, and low cognitive could participate in the same activity at the same time
6. The number of activities in the last three months tailored for high, but not medium and low, cognitive functioning residents
7. The number of activities in the past three months tailored for low, but not high and medium, cognitive functioning residents
8. The number of activities in the past three months tailored for high, but not medium and low, physical functioning residents
9. The average activity attendance of high, medium, and low physical functioning residents
10. The average activity attendance of high, medium, and low cognitive functioning residents
11. The percentage of activities offered involving each of the activities media recorded
12. The percentage of residents who had an interest in these same activities media

This information produced a framework for understanding the program's strengths and areas for improvements. Following are examples of what the data revealed. One third of the High Physical and High Cognitive Functioning residents refused to attend activities. This was contrasted with the fact that only thirteen out of three hundred activities were specifically designed for these residents. Two thirds of all the activities during the previous three months were core activities designed to meet the general needs of most residents. This high refusal rate was likely a result of not enough tailored activities.

The monthly average activity attendance during the previous three months was 8.28 for the Low Physical Functioning. For the Low Cognitive Functioning, it was 16.08. Both scores were considerably lower than the High or Medium Physical, or High or Medium Cognitive Functioning residents. This merited further exploration to determine why this happened. One possibility was the few activities tailored for Low Cognitive or Low Physical Functioning residents.

Comparing the calendar audit with the resident preferences revealed many of the program's strengths. High percentages of activities were offered in music, reading, and handwork. Low percentages of activities were scheduled in sports, hunting, and games. The frequency of these offerings was in line with the identified resident preferences.

Matching group activities to resident interests revealed some obvious areas for new programs. Intergenerational programs, gardening, and cooking were scheduled less than five percent of the time. Residents' preferences in these areas were sixty to eighty percent.

Making Changes

Gathering quality assurance data, like resident assessment, is a beginning step. Following up the findings with improvements is necessary to facilitate optimal programs. The activity staff responded to the survey results by implementing program changes. Several areas were targeted for the initial alterations.

The activity staff decided to increase tailored activities geared to meet the needs of the High and Low Physical, and High and Low Cognitive Functioning Residents. The design for each of these activities was based on Special Needs Programming as discussed in Chapter 7. All the tailored groups were small. Other departments

were notified of which residents could maximally benefit from this programming so ADLs, therapies and other services could be coordinated accordingly.

Following is a description of the tailored activities instituted for each functioning level targeted. An intensive exercise program for residents with High Physical Functioning was scheduled three times weekly. This was a joint effort of the activity staff, the physical therapy staff, and a volunteer with aerobic teaching skills. The restorative aide coordinated a three times weekly exercise program for the Low Physical Functioning. Since intergenerational programs were a common interest of High Cognitive Functioning Residents, a local church group was contacted to initiate a program involving children and these residents. This program included oral history lessons documented in a newsletter, a joint Christmas play, a talent show, and fund-raising projects. The optimum goal for this activity's frequency was one time weekly. For Low Cognitive Functioning residents, gardening was a common interest. The activity staff designed a tailored gardening program two times weekly.

The results showed that the majority of residents in the study regardless of functioning level preferred gardening, cooking, and intergenerational programs. The calendar audit showed a need to increase activity offerings in these areas. The gardening and intergenerational programs just discussed addressed part of this concern. Additional programs were implemented for residents of all functioning levels. The staff scheduled a cooking activity to meet two times monthly. This involved a variety of cooking activities including making one dish of a meal, e.g., salad, sandwich, or no bake cookies, and putting together a recipe book. Designing this activity made the staff aware of multiple cooking equipment needs. A gardening activity was scheduled two times monthly. This was to take place year-round and was to involve a wide variety of gardening projects. Equipment needs also were identified.

The activity staff established six months as a reasonable period before evaluating the results of these improvements. This evaluation will study the same residents as the first study. Group activity calendars for the three months prior to the beginning of the evaluation will be used to note changes.

Ongoing monitoring of results must permeate the program's daily tasks and exist as an expected part of every staff member's responsibility. This will lead to residents having optimal opportunities to participate in activity pursuits of their choice. There are many quality assurance methods to consider. The material here is intended to provoke a discussion of, and an interest in, the critical purpose that quality assurance serves. The reader is encouraged to use these ideas as a model from which to expand.

10 CONCLUSION

A sense of belonging, health, and enriched choices are the results of engaging in activity pursuits. These experiences begin at childbirth and continue to validate life throughout the spectrum of existence. The frail elderly, regardless of functioning deficits or living environment, require these opportunities to access the meaning of life and grapple with the inevitability of death.

Assessment begins a road of exploration and discovery that creates these opportunities. It is an unremitting process that requires perseverance and an ability to transform formal tasks into an understanding of a person's current experiences. The individual is a constant reminder of the ever changing nature of the human condition. Multiple functioning problems and diverse needs combine with individual characteristics and life patterns, making conformity of approaches impossible. The assessment detective is challenged, inspired, confused and sometimes frustrated while following this unpredictable trail.

The activity assessment is devoted to the value of activity pursuits. It collects information about how aspects of functioning and needs relate to activity involvement. Assessment identifies the impact that the current circumstances are having on an individual's desire to pursue meaningful activity. This is the beginning point for designing interventions. Adaptation is the primary strategy for reuniting an individual with optimal activity experiences.

Activity assessments form the cornerstone for program development. Once a foundation of core activity programs is built, the rewarding task of tailoring activities to meet the needs of individuals commences. Workable solutions do not come easily, but when residents' basic needs are met and they begin to seek friendship, self-esteem, and self-actualization, the activity program has come to fruition. Gratifying relationships with others, manipulation of the environment, optimal health and self-designed choices are recognizable outcomes of this achievement.

The arduous task of documentation is alleviated when it becomes a path to improved services. This path reveals truths that otherwise would remain uncovered or forgotten. Quality assurance furnishes an objective evaluation of individual results and program trends. Tracking progress furnishes the necessary tools for recognizing gains and mitigating failures.

Activity pursuits enrich our lives. Therapeutic activity programs cultivate an atmosphere that continues this enrichment for those who happen to be living in a nursing facility. Activity pursuits foster a renewal of autonomy by providing access to forgotten competencies and by inspiring of personal discoveries. The activity professional is a key player in assuring that this holistic, wellness viewpoint permeates the nursing home environment and results in improved respect for the full range of resident needs and abilities.

Chapter 10

REFERENCES

Department of Health and Human Services, Health Care Financing Administration (1989). Medicare and Medicaid: Requirements for long term care facilities; final rule with request for comment. *Federal Register*, *54*(21), pp. 5316-5373.

Department of Health and Human Services (1992). *State operations manual: Survey procedures, forms and interpretive guidelines for the long term care survey process* (Transmittal #250). Baltimore, MD: Health Care Financing Administration.

Dorlands, W. A. N. (1988). *Dorland's illustrated medical dictionary*, (27th ed.). Philadelphia, PA: W. B. Saunders Company.

Fry, P. S. (1986). *Depression, stress, and adaptations in the elderly: Psychological assessment and intervention*. Rockville, MD: Aspen Publishers, Inc.

Gibbons, A. C. (1977). Popular music preferences of elderly people. *Journal of Music Therapy*, XIV, 180-189.

Institute of Medicine (1986). *Improving the quality of care in nursing homes*. Washington, DC: National Academy Press.

Mace, N. L. and Rabins, P. V. (1981). *The 36-hour day: A family guide to caring for persons with Alzheimer's disease, related dementing illnesses and memory loss in later life*. Baltimore, MD: The Johns Hopkins University Press.

Maslow, A. H. (1968). *Toward a psychology of being*, (2nd ed.). New York, NY: Van Nostrand Reinhold.

Moore, B. (1989). *Growing with gardening: A twelve-month guide for therapy, recreation and education*. Chapel Hill, NC: University of North Carolina Press.

Morris, J. N., Hawes, C., Fries, B. E., Phillips, C. D., Mor, V., Katz, S., Murphy, K., Drugovich, M. L., and Friedlob, A. S. (1990). Designing the national resident assessment instrument for nursing homes. *The Gerontologist*, *30*(3), 293-307.

Morris, J. N., Hawes, C., Murphy, K., Nonemaker, S., Phillips, C., Fries, B. E., Mor, V. (1991). *Resident assessment instrument training manual and resource guide*. Natick, MA: Eliot Press.

Omnibus Budget Reconciliation Act of 1987: Subtitle C—Nursing Home Reform, Part 1—Medicare Program. Public Law 100-203.

Perschbacher, R. (1986). NAAP sends comments to HCFA regarding the new survey. *NAAP News*, V(5), Dec. 1986, 4.

Perschbacher, R. (1989). *Stepping forward with activities*. Asheville, NC: Bristlecone Consulting Company.

Rothert, E. A., Jr. and Daubert, J. R. (1981). *Horticultural therapy for nursing homes, senior centers, retirement living*. Glencoe, IL: Chicago Horticultural Society.

Scholtes, P. R., et. al. (1988). *The team handbook: How to use teams to improve quality*. Madison, WI: Joiner Associates, Inc.

Walz, T. H. and Blum, N. S. (1988). The age cohort factor in activities programming for the elderly. *Activities, Adaptation, and Aging*, *12*(1/2), 1-12.

APPENDIX A:
Minimum Data Set for Nursing Home Resident Assessment and Care Screening (MDS)

Appendix A-1
Minimum Data Set for Nursing Home Resident Assessment and Care Screening (MDS)
(Background Information/Intake at Admission)

I. IDENTIFICATION INFORMATION

1.	RESIDENT NAME	
		(First)　　(Middle Initial)　　(Last)

2.	DATE OF CURRENT ADMISSION	Month　　Day　　Year

3.	MEDICARE NO. (SOC. SEC. OR COMPARABLE NO. F NO MEDICARE NO.)	

4.	FACILITY PROVIDER NUMBER	Federal Number

5.	GENDER	1. Male　　　2. Female

6.	RACE/ ETHNICITY	1. American Indian/ Alaska Native　4. Hispanic 2. Asian/Pacific Islander　5. White, not of Hispanic origin 3. Black, not of Hispanic origin

7.	BIRTHDATE	Month　　Day　　Year

8.	LIFETIME OCCUPATION	

9.	PRIMARY LANGUAGE	Resident's primary language is a language other than English 0. No　　1. Yes _____ (Specify)

10.	RESIDENTIAL HISTORY PAST 5 YEARS	(Check all settings resident lived in during 5 years prior to admission)
		Prior stay at this nursing home	a.
		Other nursing home/residential facility	b.
		MH/psychiatric setting	c.
		MR/DD setting	d.
		NONE OF ABOVE	e.

11.	MENTAL HEALTH HISTORY	Does resident's RECORD indicate any history of mental retardation, mental illness, or any other mental health problem? 0. No　　1. Yes

12.	CONDITIONS RELATED TO MR/ DD STATUS	(Check all conditions that are related to MR/DD status, that were manifested before age 22, and are likely to continue indefinitely)
		Not applicable-no MR/DD (Skip to Item 13)	a.
		MR/DD with organic condition	
		Cerebral palsy	b.
		Down's syndrome	c.
		Autism	d.
		Epilepsy	e.
		Other organic condition related to MR/DD	f.
		MR/DD with no organic condition	g.
		Unknown	h.

13.	MARITAL STATUS	1. Never Married　4. Separated 2. Married　　　5. Divorced 3. Widowed

14.	ADMITTED FROM	1. Private home or apt.　3. Acute care hospital 2. Nursing home　4. Other

15.	LIVED ALONE	0. No　1. Yes　2. In other facility

16.	ADMISSION INFORMATION AMENDED	(Check all that apply)
		Accurate information unavailable earlier	a.
		Observation revealed additional information	b.
		Resident unstable at admission	c.

II. BACKGROUND INFORMATION AT RETURN/READMISSION

1.	DATE OF CURRENT READMISSION	Month　　Day　　Year

2.	MARITAL STATUS	1. Never Married　4. Separated 2. Married　　　5. Divorced 3. Widowed

3.	ADMITTED FROM	1. Private home or apt.　3. Acute care hospital 2. Nursing home　4. Other

4.	LIVED ALONE	0. No　1. Yes　2. In other facility

5.	ADMISSION INFORMATION AMENDED	(Check all that apply)
		Accurate information unavailable earlier	a.
		Observation revealed additional information	b.
		Resident unstable at admission	c.

Signature of RN Assessment Coordinator:

Signatures of Others Who Completed Part of the Assessment:

_____

_____

_____

_____

_____

_____

(Appendix A-1 Continued on Reverse Side)

Appendix A-1 (continued)
Minimum Data Set for Nursing Home Resident Assessment and Care Screening (MDS)

III. CUSTOMARY ROUTINE (ONLY AT FIRST ADMISSION)

1. CUSTOMARY ROUTINE (YEAR PRIOR TO FIRST ADMISSION TO A NURSING HOME)	(***Check all that apply.*** *If all information UNKNOWN, check last box only*)	
	CYCLE OF DAILY EVENTS	
	Stays up late at night (e.g., after 9 p.m.)	a.
	Naps regularly during day (at least 1 hour)	b.
	Goes out 1 + days a week	c.
	Stays busy with hobbies, reading, or fixed daily routine	d.
	Spends most time alone or watching TV	e.
	Moves independently indoors (with appliances, if used)	f.
	NONE OF ABOVE	g.
	EATING PATTERNS	
	Distinct food preferences	h.
	Eats between meals all or most days	i.
	Use of alcoholic beverages(s) at least weekly	j.
	NONE OF ABOVE	k.
	ADL PATTERNS	
	In bedclothes much of day	l.
	Wakens to toilet all or most nights	m.
	Has irregular bowel movement pattern	n.
	Prefers showers for bathing	o.
	NONE OF ABOVE	p.
	INVOLVEMENT PATTERNS	
	Daily contact with relatives/close friends	q.
	Usually attends church, temple, synagogue (etc.)	r.
	Finds strength in faith	s.
	Daily animal companion/presence	t.
	Involved in group activities	u.
	NONE OF ABOVE	v.
	Unknown—Resident/family unable to provide information	w.

END

Appendix A-2
Minimum Data Set for Nursing Home Resident Assessment and Care Screening (MDS)
(Status in last seven days, unless other time frame indicated)

SECTION A. IDENTIFICATION AND BACKGROUND INFORMATION

1.	ASSESSMENT DATE	Month	Day	Year

2.	RESIDENT NAME	(First) (Middle Initial) (Last)

3.	SOCIAL SECURITY No.	

4.	MEDICAID No. (IF APPLICABLE)	

5.	MEDICAL RECORD No.	

6.	REASON FOR ASSESSMENT	1. Initial admission assessment 2. Hosp/Medicare reassessment 3. Readmission assessment 4. Annual assessment 5. Significant change in status 6. Other (e.g., UR)

7. CURRENT PAYMENT SOURCE(S) FOR N.H. STAY
(Billing office to indicate; check all that apply)

Medicaid	a.	VA	d.
Medicare	b.	Self pay/	
CHAMPUS	c.	private insurance	e.
		Other	f.

8. RESPONSIBILITY/LEGAL GUARDIAN *(Check all that apply)*

Legal guardian	a.
Other legal oversight	b.
Durable power of attorney/health care proxy	c.
Family member responsible	d.
Resident responsible	e.
NONE OF ABOVE	f.

9. ADVANCED DIRECTIVES *(For those items with supporting documentation in the medical record, check all that apply)*

Living will	a.
Do not resuscitate	b.
Do not hospitalize	c.
Organ donation	d.
Autopsy request	e.
Feeding restrictions	f.
Medication restrictions	g.
Other treatment restrictions	h.
NONE OF ABOVE	i.

10.	DISCHARGE PLANNED WITHIN 3 MOS.	*(Does not include discharge due to death)* 0. No 1. Yes 2. Unknown/uncertain

11.	PARTICIPATE IN ASSESSMENT	a. Resident 0. No 1. Yes	b. Family 0. No 1. Yes 2. No family	a. b.

12. SIGNATURES

Signature of RN Assessment Coordinator

Signatures of others who completed part of the assessment

_____   _____

_____   _____

_____

SECTION B. COGNITIVE PATTERNS

1.	COMATOSE	*(Persistent vegetative state/no discernible consciousness)* 0. No 1. Yes **(Skip to Section E)**	

2.	MEMORY	*(Recall of what was learned or known)* a. Short-term memory OK— seems/appears to recall after 5 minutes 0. Memory OK 1. Memory problem	a.
		b. Long-term memory OK— seems/appears to recall long past 0. Memory OK 1. Memory problem	b.

3.	MEMORY/RECALL ABILITY	*(**Check** all that resident normally is able to recall during last 7 days)*	
		Current season	a.
		Location of own room	b.
		Staff names/faces	c.
		That he/she is in a nursing home	d.
		None of Above are recalled	e.

4.	COGNITIVE SKILLS FOR DAILY DECISION MAKING	*(Made decisions regarding tasks of daily life)* 0. Independent— decisions consistent/reasonable 1. Modified independence— some difficulty in new situations only 2. Moderately impaired— decisions poor; cues/supervision required 3. Severely impaired— never/rarely made decisions	

5.	INDICATORS OF DELIRIUM—PERIODIC DISORDERED THINKING/AWARENESS	*(**Check** if condition over last 7 days appears different from usual functioning)*	
		Less alert, easily distracted	a.
		Changing awareness of environment	b.
		Episodes of incoherent speech	c.
		Periods of motor restlessness or lethargy	d.
		Cognitive ability varies over course of day	e.
		NONE OF ABOVE	f.

6.	CHANGE IN COGNITIVE STATUS	Change in resident's cognitive status, skills, or abilities in **last 90 days** 0. No change 1. Improved 2. Deteriorated	

Code the appropriate response = ▨

Check all the responses that apply = ☐

(Appendix A-2 Continued on Reverse Side)

Appendix A-2 (continued)
Minimum Data Set for Nursing Home Resident Assessment and Care Screening (MDS)
(Status in last seven days, unless other time frame indicated)

SECTION C. COMMUNICATION/HEARING PATTERNS

1.	Hearing	*(With hearing applicance, if used)* 0. Hears adequately—normal talk, TV, phone 1. Minimal difficulty when not in quiet setting 2. Hears in special situations only—speaker has to adjust tonal quality and speak distinctly 3. Highly impaired/absence of useful hearing	
2.	Communi-cation Devices/ Techniques	*(**Check all that apply** during last 7 days)* Hearing aid, present and used a. Hearing aid, present and not used b. Other receptive comm. techniques used (e.g., lip read) c. NONE OF ABOVE d.	
3.	Modes of Expression	*(**Check all used** by resident to make needs known)* Speech a. Writing messages to express or clarify needs b. Signs/gestures/sounds c. Communication board d. Other e. NONE OF ABOVE f.	
4.	Making Self Understood	(Express information content—however able) 0 Understood 1. Usually understood—difficulty finding words or finishing thoughts 2. Sometimes understood—ability is limited to making concrete requests 3. Rarely/Never Understood	
5.	Ability to Understand Others	*(Understanding verbal information content—however able)* 0. Understands 1. Usually understands—may miss some part/intent of message 2. Sometimes understands—responds adequately to simple, direct communication 3. Rarely/Never Understands	
6.	Change in Communi-cation/ Hearing	Resident's ability to express, understand, or hear information has changed over **last 90 days** 0. No change 1. Improved 2. Deteriorated	

SECTION D. VISION PATTERNS

1.	Vision	*(Ability to see in adequate light and with glasses, if used)* 0. Adequate—sees fine detail, including regular print in newspapers/books 1. Impaired—sees large print, but not regular print in newspapers/books 2. Highly impaired—limited vision; not able to see newspaper headlines; appears to follow objects with eyes 3. Severely impaired—no vision or appears to see only light, colors, or shapes	
2.	Visual Limitations/ Difficulties	Side vision problems—decreased peripheral vision (e.g., leaves food on one side of tray, difficulty traveling, bumps into people and objects, misjudges placement of chair when seating self) a. Experiences any of following: sees halos or rings around lights; sees flashes of light; sees "curtains" over eyes b. NONE OF ABOVE c.	
3.	Visual Appliances	Glasses; contact lenses; lens implant; magnifying glass 0. No 1. Yes	

Code the appropriate response = ▨

Check all the responses that apply = ☐

Appendix A-3
Minimum Data Set for Nursing Home Resident Assessment and Care Screening (MDS)
(Status in last seven days, unless other time frame indicated)

SECTION E. PHYSICAL FUNCTIONING AND STRUCTURAL PROBLEMS

1. ADL Self-performance—(***Code** for resident's **PERFORMANCE OVER ALL SHIFTS** During Last 7 days—Not including setup*)

0. INDEPENDENT—No help or oversight—OR—Help/ oversight provided only 1 or 2 times during last 7 days

1. SUPERVISION—Oversight, encouragement, or cueing provided 3+ times during last 7 days—OR—Supervision plus physical assistance provided only 1 or 2 times during last 7 days

2. LIMITED ASSISTANCE—Resident highly involved in activity; received physical help in guided maneuvering of limbs or other nonweight bearing assistance 3+ times—OR— More help provided only 1 or 2 times during last 7 days

3. EXTENSIVE ASSISTANCE—While resident performed part of activity, over last 7-day period, help of following type(s) provided 3 or more times:
_____ Weight-bearing support
_____ Full staff performance during part (but not all) of last 7 days

4. TOTAL DEPENDENCE—Full staff performance of activity during entire 7 days

2. ADL Support Provided—(***Code** for **MOST SUPPORT PROVIDED OVER ALL SHIFTS** During Last 7 Days; **Code** **Regardless** of resident's self-performance classification*)

0. No setup or physical help from staff
1. Setup help only
2. One-person physical assist
3. Two+ persons physical assist

			(1) Self-performance	(2) Support
a.	BED MOBILITY	How resident moves to and from lying position, turns side-to-side, and positions body while in bed		
b.	TRANSFER	How resident moves between surfaces—to/from: bed, chair, wheelchair, standing position (Exclude to/ from bath/toilet)		
c.	LOCOMOTION	How resident moves between locations in his/her room and adjacent corridor on same floor. If in wheelchair, self-sufficiency once in chair.		
d.	DRESSING	How resident puts on, fastens, and takes off all items of street clothing, including donning/removing prosthesis		
e.	EATING	How resident eats and drinks (regardless of skill)		
f.	TOILET USE	How resident uses the toilet room (or commode, bedpan, urinal); transfer on/off toilet, cleanses, changes pad, manages ostomy or catheter, adjusts clothes		
g.	PERSONAL HYGIENE	How resident maintains personal hygiene, including combing hair, brushing teeth, shaving, applying makeup, washing/drying face, hands, and perineum (EXCLUDE baths and showers)		

Code the appropriate response(s) = ▨
Check all responses that apply = ☐

3. BATHING — How resident takes full-body bath/shower, sponge bath and transfers in/out of tub/shower (**EXCLUDE** *washing of back and hair.* **CODE FOR MOST DEPENDENT** *in self-performance and support. Bathing Self-performance codes appear below*)

	(1) a. Self-performance	(2) b. Support
0. Independent—No help provided		
1. Supervision—Oversight help only		
2. Physical help limited to transfer only		
3. Physical help in part of bathing activity		
4. Total dependence		

4. BODY CONTROL PROBLEMS — (***Check all that apply** during last 7 days*)

Balance—partial or total loss of ability to balance self while standing	a.
Bedfast all or most of the time	b.
Contracture to arms, legs, shoulders, or hands	c.
Hemiplegia/hemiparesis	d.
Quadriplegia	e.
Arm—partial or total loss of voluntary movement	f.
Hand—lack of dexterity (e.g., problem using toothbrush or adjusting hearing aid)	g.
Leg—partial or total loss of voluntary movement	h.
Leg—unsteady gait	i.
Trunk—partial or total loss of ability to position, balance, or turn body	j.
Amputation	k.
None of Above	l.

5. MOBILITY APPLIANCES/ DEVICES — (***Check all that apply** during last 7 days*)

Cane/walker	a.	Other person wheeled	d.
Brace/prosthesis	b.	Lifted (manually/ mechanically)	e.
Wheeled self	c.	NONE OF ABOVE	f.

6. TASK SEGMENTATION — Resident requires that some or all of ADL activities be broken into a series of subtasks so that resident can perform them

0. No   1. Yes

7. ADL FUNCTIONAL REHABILITATION POTENTIAL

Resident believes he/she capable of increased independence in at least some ADLs	a.
Direct care staff believe resident capable of increased independence in at least some ADLs	b.
Resident able to perform tasks/activity but is very slow	c.
Major difference in ADL Self-Performance or ADL Support in mornings and evenings (at least a one category change in Self-Performance or Support in any ADL)	d.
None of Above	e.

8. CHANGE IN ADL FUNCTION — Change in ADL self-performance in **last 90 days**

0. No change   1. Improved   2. Deteriorated

(Appendix A-3 Continued on Reverse Side)

Appendix A-3 (continued)
Minimum Data Set for Nursing Home Resident Assessment and Care Screening (MDS)
(Status in last seven days, unless other time frame indicated)

SECTION F. CONTINENCE IN LAST 14 DAYS

1.   Continence Self-Control Categories
(**Code** for resident performance over all shifts)
   0. **CONTINENT**—Complete control
   1. **USUALLY CONTINENT**—Bladder, incontinent episodes once a week or less; bowel, less than weekly
   2. **OCCASIONALLY INCONTINENT**—Bladder, 2+ times a week but not daily; bowel, once a week
   3. **FREQUENTLY INCONTINENT**—Bladder, tended to be incontinent daily, but some control present (e.g., on day shift); bowel, 2-3 times a week
   4. **INCONTINENT**—Had inadequate control. Bladder, multiple daily episodes; bowel, all (or almost all) of the time

a.	**Bowel Continence**	Control of bowel movement, with appliance or bowel continence programs, if employed	
b.	**Bladder Continence**	Control of urinary bladder function (if dribbles, volume insufficient to soak through underpants), with appliances (e.g., foley) or continence programs, if employed	
2.	**INCONTINENCE RELATED TESTING**	*(Skip if resident's bladder continence code equals 0 or 1 and no catheter is used)*	
		Resident has been tested for a urinary tract infection	a.
		Resident has been checked for presence of fecal impaction, or there is adequate bowel elimination	b.
		NONE OF ABOVE	c.
3.	**APPLIANCES AND PROGRAMS**	Any scheduled toileting plan	a.
		External (condom) catheter	b.
		Indwelling catheter	c.
		Intermittent catheter	d.
		Did not use toilet room/commode/urinal	e.
		Pads/briefs used	f.
		Enemas/irrigation	g.
		Ostomy	h.
		NONE OF ABOVE	i.
4.	**CHANGE IN URINARY CONTINENCE**	Change in urinary continence/appliances and programs in **last 90 days** 0. No Change 1. Improved 2. Deteriorated	

Code the appropriate response(s) = ▢
Check all the responses that apply = ▢

SECTION G. PSYCHOSOCIAL WELL-BEING

1.	**SENSE OF INITIATIVE/ INVOLVEMENT**	At ease interacting with others	a.
		At ease doing planned or structured activities	b.
		At ease doing self-initiated activities	c.
		Establishes own goals	d.
		Pursues involvement in life of facility (e.g., makes/keeps friends; involved in group activities; responds positively to new activities; assists at religious services)	e.
		Accepts invitations into most group activities	f.
		NONE OF ABOVE	g.
2.	**UNSETTLED RELATIONSHIPS**	Covert/open conflict with and/or repeated criticism of staff	a.
		Unhappy with roommate	b.
		Unhappy with residents other than roommate	c.
		Openly expresses conflict/anger with family or friends	d.
		Absence of personal contact with family/friends	e.
		Recent loss of close family member/ friend	f.
		NONE OF ABOVE	g.
3.	**PAST ROLES**	Strong identification with past roles and life status	a.
		Expresses sadness/anger/empty feeling over lost roles/status	b.
		NONE OF ABOVE	c.

Appendix A-4
Minimum Data Set for Nursing Home Resident Assessment and Care Screening (MDS)
(Status in last seven days, unless other time frame indicated)

SECTION H. MOOD AND BEHAVIOR PATTERNS

1. SAD OR ANXIOUS MOOD	(*Check all that apply* during last 30 days)	
	Verbal Expressions of Distress by resident (sadness, sense that nothing matters, hopelessness, worthlessness, unrealistic fears, vocal expressions of anxiety or grief)	a.
	DEMONSTRATED (OBSERVABLE) SIGNS OF MENTAL DISTRESS Tearfulness, emotional groaning, sighing, breathlessness	b.
	Motor agitation such as pacing, handwringing, or picking	c.
	Failure to eat or take medications, withdrawal from self-care or leisure activities	d.
	Pervasive concern with health	e.
	Recurrent thoughts of death—e.g., believes he/she about to die, have a heart attack	f.
	Suicidal thoughts/actions	g.
	NONE OF ABOVE	h.

2. MOOD PERSISTENCE	Sad or anxious mood intrudes on daily life over **last 7 days**—not easily altered, doesn't "cheer up" 0. No 1. Yes	

3. PROBLEM BEHAVIOR	(*Code for behavior* in last 7 days) 0. Behavior not exhibited in last 7 days 1. Behavior of this type occurred less than daily 2. Behavior of this type occurred daily or more frequently	
	WANDERING (moved with no rational purpose, seemingly oblivious to needs or safety)	a.
	VERBALLY ABUSIVE (others were threatened, screamed at, cursed at)	b.
	PHYSICALLY ABUSIVE (others were hit, shoved, scratched, sexually abused)	c.
	SOCIALLY INAPPROPRIATE/DISRUPTIVE BEHAVIOR (made disrupting sounds, noisy, screams, self-abusive acts, sexual behavior or disrobing in public, smeared/threw food/feces, hoarding, rummaged through others' belongings)	d.

4. RESIDENT RESISTS CARE	(*Check all types of resistance* that occurred in the last 7 days)	
	Resisted taking medications/injections	a.
	Resisted ADL assistance	b.
	NONE OF ABOVE	c.

5. BEHAVIOR MANAGEMENT PROGRAM	Behavior problem has been addressed by clinically developed behavior management program. (Note: Do not include programs that involve only physical restraints or psychotropic medications in this category) 0. No behavior problem 1. Yes, addressed 2. No, not addressed	

6. CHANGE IN MOOD	Change in mood in **last 90 days** 0. No change 1. Improved 2. Deteriorated	

7. CHANGE IN PROBLEM BEHAVIOR	Change in problem behavioral signs in **last 90 days** 0. No change 1. Improved 2. Deteriorated	

SECTION I. ACTIVITY PURSUIT PATTERNS

1. TIME AWAKE	(*Check appropriate time periods* over last 7 days) Resident awake all or most of time (i.e., naps no more than one hour per time period) in the:	
	Morning	a.
	Afternoon	b.
	Evening	c.
	None of Above	d.

2. AVERAGE TIME INVOLVED IN ACTIVITIES	0. Most—more than 2/3 of time 1. Some—1/3 to 2/3 of time 2. Little—less than 1/3 of time 3. None	

3. PREFERRED ACTIVITY SETTINGS	(*Check all settings* in which activities are preferred)	
	Own room	a.
	Day/activity room	b.
	Inside NH/off unit	c.
	Outside facility	d.
	NONE OF ABOVE	e.

4. GENERAL ACTIVITY PREFERENCES (ADAPTED TO RESIDENT'S CURRENT ABILITIES)	(*Check all preferences* whether or not activity is currently available to resident)	
	Cards/other games	a.
	Crafts/arts	b.
	Exercise/sports	c.
	Music	d.
	Read/write	e.
	Spiritual/religious activities	f.
	Trips/shopping	g.
	Walking/wheeling outdoors	h.
	Watch TV	i.
	NONE OF ABOVE	j.

5. PREFERS MORE OR DIFFERENT ACTIVITIES	Resident expresses/indicates preference for other activities/choices 0. No 1. Yes	

Code the appropriate response(s) = ▨
Check all the responses that apply = ☐

(Appendix A-4 Continued on Reverse Side)

Appendix A-4 (continued)
Minimum Data Set for Nursing Home Resident Assessment and Care Screening (MDS)
(Status in last seven days, unless other time frame indicated)

SECTION J. DISEASE DIAGNOSES

CHECK ONLY THOSE DISEASES PRESENT THAT HAVE A RELATIONSHIP to current ADL status, cognitive status, behavior status, medical treatments, or risk of death (Do not list old/inactive diagnoses)

1. Diseases	(If none apply, check the None of Above box)	
	HEART/CIRCULATION	
	Arteriosclerotic heart disease (ASHD)	a.
	Cardiac dysrhythmias	b.
	Congestive heart failure	c.
	Hypertension	d.
	Hypotension	e.
	Peripheral vascular disease	f.
	Other cardiovascular disease	g.
	NEUROLOGICAL	
	Alzheimer's	h.
	Dementia other than Alzheimer's	i.
	Aphasia	j.
	Cerebrovascular accident (stroke)	k.
	Multiple sclerosis	l.
	Parkinson's disease	m.
	PULMONARY	
	Emphysema/Asthma/COPD	n.
	Pneumonia	o.
	PSYCHIATRIC/MOOD	
	Anxiety disorder	p.
	Depression	q.
	Manic depressive (bipolar disease)	r.
	SENSORY	
	Cataracts	s.
	Glaucoma	t.
	OTHER	
	Allergies	u.
	Anemia	v.
	Arthritis	w.
	Cancer	x.
	Diabetes mellitus	y.
	Explicit terminal prognosis	z.
	Hypothyroidism	aa.
	Osteoporosis	bb.
	Seizure disorder	cc.
	Septicemia	dd.
	Urinary tract infection **in last 30 days**	ee.
	None of Above	ff.

2. OTHER CURRENT DIAGNOSES AND ICD-9 CODES	a. _____
	b. _____
	c. _____
	d. _____
	e. _____
	f. _____

SECTION K. HEALTH CONDITIONS

1. PROBLEM CONDITIONS	(*Check all problems* that are present in last 7 days unless other time frame indicated)	
	Constipation	a.
	Diarrhea	b.
	Dizziness/vertigo	c.
	Edema	d.
	Fecal impaction	e.
	Fever	f.
	Hallucinations/delusions	g.
	Internal bleeding	h.
	Joint pain	i.
	Pain—resident complains or shows evidence of pain daily or almost daily	j.
	Recurrent lung aspirations in **last 90 days**	k.
	Shortness of breath	l.
	Syncope (fainting)	m.
	Vomiting	n.
	NONE OF ABOVE	o.

2. ACCIDENTS		
	Fell in **past 30 days**	a.
	Fell in **past 31-180 days**	b.
	Hip fracture in **last 180 days**	c.
	NONE OF ABOVE	d.

3. STABILITY OF CONDITIONS		
	Conditions/diseases make resident's cognitive, ADL or behavior status unstable—fluctuating, precarious, or deteriorating	a.
	Resident experiencing an acute episode or a flare-up of a recurrent chronic problem	b.
	NONE OF ABOVE	c.

Appendix A-5
Minimum Data Set for Nursing Home Resident Assessment and Care Screening (MDS)
(Status in last seven days, unless other time frame indicated)

SECTION L. ORAL/NUTRITIONAL STATUS

1. ORAL PROBLEMS	Chewing problem	a.
	Swallowing problem	b.
	Mouth pain	c.
	None of Above	d.

2. HEIGHT AND WEIGHT	Record height (**a.**) in inches and weight (**b.**) in pounds. Weight based on most recent status in **last 30 days**; measure weight consistently in accord with standard facility practice—e.g., in a.m. after voiding, before meal, with shoes off, and in nightclothes.	
	(a.) HT (in.) (b.) WT (lbs.)	
	c. weight loss (i.e., 5% in **last 30 days**; or 10% in **last 180 days**) 0. No 1. Yes	

3. NUTRITIONAL PROBLEMS	Complains about the taste of many foods	a.
	Insufficient fluid; dehydrated	b.
	Did **NOT** consume all/almost all liquids provided **during last 3 days**	c.
	Regular complaint of hunger	d.
	Leaves 25%+ food uneaten at most meals	e.
	NONE OF ABOVE	f.

4. NUTRITIONAL APPROACHES	Parenteral/IV	a.
	Feeding tube	b.
	Mechanically-altered diet	c.
	Syringe (oral feeding)	d.
	Therapeutic diet	e.
	Dietary supplement between meals	f.
	Plate guard, stabilized built-up utensil, etc	g.
	NONE OF ABOVE	h.

SECTION M. ORAL/DENTAL STATUS

1. ORAL STATUS AND DISEASE PREVENTION	Debris (soft, easily movable substances) present in mouth prior to going to bed at night	a.
	Has dentures and/or removeable bridge	b.
	Some/all natural teeth lost—does not have or does not use dentures (or partial plates)	c.
	Broken, loose or carious teeth	d.
	Inflamed gums (gingiva); swollen or bleeding gums; oral abscesses, ulcers, or rashes	e.
	Daily cleaning of teeth/dentures	f.
	NONE OF ABOVE	g.

SECTION N. SKIN CONDITION

| 1. STASIS ULCER | Open lesion caused by poor venous circulation to lower extremities   0. No   1. Yes | |

2. PRESSURE ULCERS	(***Code for highest stage*** of pressure ulcer)	
	0. No pressure ulcer	
	1. Stage 1: A persistent area of skin redness (without a break in the skin) that does not disappear when pressure is relieved	
	2. Stage 2: A partial thickness loss of skin layers that presents clinically as an abrasion, blister, or shallow crater	
	3. Stage 3: A full thickness of skin is lost, exposing the subcutaneous tissues—presents as a deep crater with or without undermining adjacent tissue	
	4. Stage 4: A full thickness of skin and subcutaneous tissue is lost, exposing muscle and/or bone	

| 3. HISTORY OF RESOLVED/CURED PRESSURE ULCERS | Resident has had a pressure ulcer that was resolved/cured in **last 90 days**   0. No   1. Yes | |

4. SKIN PROBLEMS/ CARE	Open lesions other than statis or pressure ulcers (e.g., cuts)	a.
	Skin desensitized to pain, pressure, discomfort	b.
	Protective/preventive skin care	c.
	Turning/repositioning program	d.
	Pressure relieving beds, bed/chair pads (e.g., egg crate pads)	e.
	Wound care/treatment (e.g., pressure ulcer care, surgical wound)	f.
	Other skin care/treatment	g.
	NONE OF ABOVE	h.

Code the appropriate response(s) = ▨
Check all the responses that apply = ☐

(Appendix A-5 Continued on Reverse Side)

Appendix A-5 (continued)
Minimum Data Set for Nursing Home Resident Assessment and Care Screening (MDS)
(Status in last seven days, unless other time frame indicated)

SECTION O. MEDICATION USE

1.	NUMBER OF MEDICATIONS	(*Record the number of different medications used in the last 7 days; enter "0" if none used*)	
2.	NEW MEDICATIONS	Resident has received new medications during the **last 90 days** 0. No 1. Yes	
3.	INJECTIONS	(*Record the number of days injections of any type received during the last 7 days*)	
4.	DAYS RECEIVED THE FOLLOWING MEDICATIONS	(*Record the number of days during last 7 days; enter "0" if not used; enter "1" if long-acting medications used less than weekly*) Antipsychotics a. Antianxiety/hypnotics b. Antidepressants c.	
5.	PREVIOUS MEDICATION RESULTS	(*Skip this question if resident currently receiving antipsychotics, antidepressants, or antianxiety/hypnotics—otherwise code correct response for last 90 days*) Resident has previously received psychoactive medications for a mood or behavior problem, and these medications were effective (without undue adverse consequences) 0. No, drugs not used 1. Drugs were effective 2. Drugs were not effective 3. Drug effectiveness unknown	

SECTION P. SPECIAL TREATMENT AND PROCEDURES

1.	SPECIAL TREATMENTS AND PROCEDURES	**SPECIAL CARE—Check** treatments received during the last 14 days
		Chemotherapy a. IV Medications f. Radiation b. Transfusions g. Dialysis c. O_2 h. Suctioning d. Other _____ i. Trach. care e. NONE OF ABOVE j.
		THERAPIES—Record the number of days each of the following therapies was administered (for at least 10 minutes during a day) in the last 7 days: Speech—language pathology and audiology services k. Occupational therapy l. Physical therapy m. Psychological therapy (any licensed professional) n. Respiratory therapy o.
2.	ABNORMAL LAB VALUES	Has the resident had any abnormal lab values during the **last 90 days**? 0. No 1. Yes 2. No tests performed
3.	DEVICES AND RESTRAINTS	Use the following **codes** for last 7 days: **0.** Not used **1.** Used less than daily **2.** Used daily Bed rails a. Trunk restraint b. Limb restraint c. Chair prevents rising d.

 **APPENDIX B:**
Resident Assessment Protocol: Activities

I. PROBLEM

The Activities RAP targets residents that may need a revised activity care plan to identify inactivity that may be a major complication in their lives. Resident capabilities may not be fully recognized; they may have recently moved into the facility or staff may have focused too heavily on the instrumental needs of the resident and may have lost sight of complications in the institutional environment.

Resident involvement in passive, as well as active, activities can be as important in the nursing home as it was in the community. The capabilities of the average resident have obviously been altered as abilities and expectations change, disease intervenes, situational opportunities become less frequent, and extended social relationships less common. But something that should never be overlooked is the great variability within the resident population; many will have ADL deficits, but few will be totally dependent; impaired cognition will be widespread, but so will the ability to apply old skills and learn new ones; and sense may be impaired, but some type of two-way communication is almost always possible.

For the nursing home, activity planning is a universal need. For this RAP, the focus is on cases where the system may have failed the resident, or where the resident has distressing conditions that warrant review of the activity care plan. The types of cases that will be triggered are: (1) residents who have indicated a desire for additional activity choices; (2) cognitively intact, distressed residents who may benefit from an enriched activity program; (3) cognitively deficient, distressed residents whose activity levels should be evaluated; and (4) highly involved residents whose health may be in jeopardy because of their failure to "slow down."

In evaluating triggered cases, the following general questions may be helpful:

- Is inactivity disproportionate to the resident's physical/cognitive abilities or limitations?
- Have decreased demands of nursing home life removed the need to make decisions, to set schedules, to meet challenges? Have these changes contributed to resident apathy?
- What is the nature of the naturally occurring physical and mental challenges the resident experiences in everyday life?
- In what activities is the resident involved? Is he/she normally an active participant in the life of the unit? Is the resident reserved, but actively aware of what is going on around him/her? Or is he/she unaware of surroundings and activities that take place?
- Are there proven ways to extend the resident's inquisitive/active engagement in activities?
- Might simple staff actions expedite resident involvement in activities? For example: Can equipment be modified to permit greater resident access of the unit? Can the resident's location or position be changed to permit greater access to people, views, or programs? Can time and/or distance limitations for activities be made less demanding without destroying the challenge? Can staff modes of interacting with the resident be more accommodating, possibly less threatening, to resident deficits?

Source: Morris, J. N., Hawes, C., Murphy, K., Nonemaker, S., Phillips, C., Fries, B. E., Mor, V. (1991). *Resident Assessment Instrument Training Manual and Resource Guide.* Natick, MA: Eliot Press.

II. TRIGGERS

The following sets of MDS–based conditions indicate those residents who will require further review, as well as the types of the action that may be required:

1. Revised activity plan suggested if:

    Resident Prefers More or Different Activity choices [**I5 = 1**]

2. Revised activity care plan suggested to help resident overcome resident distress when ALL THREE of the following conditions are met:

    a. *Little/No* involvement in activities [**I2 = 2 or 3**]

    b. *One/More* of following indicators of *Distress:*
        - Unsettled relationships in any area [**G2a, G2b, G2c, G2d = Any checked**]
        - Sadness over lost roles/status [**G3b = checked**]
        - Verbal expressions of sad mood **H1a = checked**]
        - Withdrawn—as indicated by complete absence of General Activity Preferences [**I4j = checked**]

    c. Two or more of following indicators of Communication/Cognitive Ability:
        - Short-term memory OK [**B2a = 0**]
        - At least some decision-making ability [**B4 = 0, 1, or 2**]
        - Understood/usually understood by others [**C4 = 0 or 1**]
        - Understood/usually understands others [**C5 = 0 or 1**]

3. Review of activity care plan to determine if its modification might help to overcome resident distress when either of the following conditions are met:
    - -a- and -b- conditions above AND resident is bedfast [**E4b =checked**]

    - -a- and -b- conditions above AND resident has *No or Only One* of the four indicators of Communication/Cognitive ability (c. above).

4. Review of activity care plan suggested if: Most involvement in activities [**I2 = 0**] *AND* two or more checked in measurement of time awake [**I1a, I1b, I1c = more than 1 checked**]

III. GUIDELINES

The follow-up review looks for factors that may impede resident involvement in activities. Although many factors can play a role, age as a valid impediment to participation can normally be ruled out. If age continues to be linked as a major cause of lack of participation, a staff education program may prove effective remedying what may be overprotective staff behavior.

Is Resident Suitably Challenged, Overstimulated? To some extent, competence depends on environmental demands. When the challenge is not sufficiently demanding, a resident can become bored, perhaps withdrawn, may resort to fault-finding and perhaps even behave mischievously to relieve the boredom. Eventually, such a resident may become less competent because of the lack of challenge. In contrast, when the resident lacks the competence to meet challenges presented by the surroundings, he or she may react with anger and aggressiveness.

- Do available activities correspond to resident lifetime values, attitudes, and expectations?
- Does resident consider "leisure activities" a waste of time—he/she never really learned to play, or to do things just for enjoyment?
- Have the resident's wishes and prior activity patterns been considered by activity and nursing professionals?

- Have staff considered how activities requiring lower energy levels may be of interest to the resident—e.g., reading a book, talking with family and friends, watching the world go by, knitting?
- Does the resident have cognitive/functional deficits that either reduce options or preclude involvement in all/most activities that would otherwise have been of interest to him/her?

Health-related factors that may affect participation in activities. Diminished cardiac output, an acute illness, reduced energy reserves, and impaired respiratory function are some of the many reasons that may cause the activity level to decline. Most of these conditions need not necessarily incapacitate the resident. All too often, disease-induced reduction of activity may lead to progressive decline through disuse and thus further decrease in activity levels. However, this pattern can be broken; many activities can be continued if they are adapted to require less exertion or if the resident is helped in adapting to a lost limb, decreased communication skills, new appliances, and so forth.

- Is resident suffering from an acute health problem?
- Is resident hindered because of embarrassment/unease due to the presence of health-related equipment (tubes, oxygen tank, colostomy bag, wheelchair)?
- Has the resident recovered from an illness? Is the capacity for participation in activities greater?
- Has an illness left the resident with some disability (e.g., slurred speech, necessity for use of cane/walker/wheelchair, limited use of hands)?
- Does resident's treatment regimen allow little time or energy for participation in preferred activities?

Recent decline in resident status—cognition, communication, function, mood, or behavior. When pathologic changes occur in any aspect of the resident's competence, the pleasurable challenge of activities may narrow. Of special interest are problematic changes that may be related to the use of psychoactive medications. When residents or staff overreact to such losses, compensatory strategies may be helpful—e.g., impaired residents may benefit from periods of both activity and rest; task segmentation can be considered; or available resident energies can be reserved for pleasurable activities (e.g., using usual stamina reserves to walk to the card room rather than to the bathroom) or activities that have individual significance (e.g., sitting unattended at a daily prayer service rather than at a group activity program).

- Has staff or the resident been overprotective? Or have they misread the seriousness of resident cognitive/functional decline? In what ways?
- Has the resident retained skills, or the capacity to learn new skills, sufficient to permit greater activity involvement?
- Does staff know what the resident was like prior to the most recent decline? Has the physician or other staff offered a prognosis for the resident's future recovery, or change of continued decline?
- Is there any substantial reason to believe that the resident cannot tolerate or would be harmed by increased activity levels? What reasons support a counter opinion?
- Does resident retain any desire to learn or master a specific new activity? Is this realistic?
- Has there been a lack of participation in the majority of activities which he/she stated as preference areas, even though these types of activities are provided?

Environmental factors. Environmental factors include recent changes in resident location, facility rules, season of the year, and physical space limitations that hinder effective resident involvement.

- Does the interplay of personal, social, and physical aspects of the facility's environment hamper involvement in activities? How might this be addressed?
- Are current activity levels affected by the season of the year or the nature of the weather during the MDS assessment period?
- Can the resident choose to participate in or to create an activity? How is this influenced by facility rules?
- Does resident prefer to be with others, but the physical layout of the unit gets in the way? Do other features in the physical plant frustrate the resident's desire to be involved in the life of the facility? What corrective actions are possible? Have any been taken?

Changes in availability of family/friends/ staff support. Many residents will experience not only a change in residence but also a loss of relationships. When this occurs, staff may wish to consider ways for a resident to develop a supportive relationship with another resident, staff member or volunteer that may increase the desire to socialize with others and/or to attend and/or participate in activities with this new friend.

- Has a staff person who has been instrumental in involving a resident in activities left the facility/been reassigned?
- Is a new member in a group activity viewed by a resident as taking over?
- Has another resident who was a leader on the unit died or left the unit?
- Is resident shy, unable to make new friends?

- Does resident's expression of dissatisfaction with fellow residents indicate he/she does not want to be a part of an activities group?

Possible Confounding Problems to be Considered for Those Now Actively Involved in Activities. Of special interest are cardiac and other diseases that might suggest a need to slow down.

ACTIVITIES RAP KEY

TRIGGERS

1. Revised activity plan suggested if: Resident Prefers More or Different Activity Choices [I5 = 1]

2. Revised activity plan suggested to help resident overcome distress if ALL of the following:
   a. Little or no involvement in activities [I2 = 2 or 3]
   b. Distress: Any indicators of unsettled relationships [G2a, G2b, G2c, G2d = any checked] OR Sadness over lost roles/status [G3b = checked] OR Verbal expressions of sad mood [H1a = checked] OR Absence of general activity preferences [I4j = checked]
   c. Two or more indicators of intact Communication and/or Cognitive Ability:
      — Short-term memory OK [B2a = 0]
      — Some decision-making ability [B4 = 0, 1 or 2]
      — Understood/usually understood by others [C4 = 0 or 1]
      — Understands/usually understands others [C5 = 0 or 1]

3. Revised activity plan suggested to determine whether modifications might help resident overcome distress if all of the following:
   a. Little or no involvement in activities [I2 = 2 or 3]

b. Distress: Two or more indicators of unsettled relationships **[G2a, G2b, G2c, G2d = two or more checked] OR** Sadness over lost roles/status **[G3b = checked] OR** Verbal expressions of sad mood **[H1a = checked] OR** Absence of general activity preferences **[I4j = checked]**

c. Resident is bedfast **[E4b = checked] OR** *None or Only One* indicator of intact Communication and/or Cognitive Ability:
   — Short-term memory OK **[B2a = 0]**
   — Some decision-making ability **[B4 = 0, 1 or 2]**
   — Understood/usually understood by others **[C4 = 0 or 1]**
   — Understands/usually understands others **[C5 = 0 or 1]**

4. Review of activity plan suggested if: Resident has most time involvement in activities **[I2 = 0] AND** is awake all or most of time **[I1a, I1b, I1c = more than 1 checked]**

GUIDELINES

Problems to be considered as activity plan is developed:

1. Cognitive status **[B]**
2. Unstable/acute health conditions **[K3]**
3. Number of treatments received **[P1]**
4. Time in facility **[INTAKE I2]**
5. Use of psychoactive medications **[O4]**

Confounding problems to be considered:
Cardiac dysrhythmias **[J1b]**, Hypertension **[J1d]**, CVA **[J1k]**

APPENDIX C:
National Association of Activity Professionals
Standards of Practice

Section A
Standards of Care

STANDARD 1

The collection of information about the past, present, and future interests as well as the values/characteristics/traits/individuality of the client/resident is systematic and continuous. The information is recorded, communicated, and accessible.

Rationale:
To be meaningful and realistic, programs must be based on a person's past and present lifestyle, interests, values, and capabilities. The client/resident must be the primary source of information to the extent possible.

Criteria:
1. Activities information should include:
   Family history
   Ethnic and cultural background
   Educational background
   Social habits (large and small groups, alone)
   Vocational background
   Recreational interests/hobbies (talents, sports, games, travel, reading, television, and fine arts)
   Membership in clubs/organizations (leadership positions)
   Volunteer activities
   Political involvement (voting habits)
   Spiritual activities (church attendance, roles, scripture study)
   Past profile of typical day/week
   Future profile (what client/resident wants within the facility)
   Life goals/aspirations/dreams
   Levels of participation; supportive, maintenance, and empowerment activity programs

2. Information is collected by the Activity Professional from:
   Client/resident
   Records and reports
   Other professionals directly involved in the care of the client/resident
   Family, significant others
3. Information is obtained from:
   Interviews
   Observation
   Reading records and reports
4. There is a format for the collection of information which is:
   Systematic
   Coordinated with information/data from all other professionals directly involved with the care of the client/resident
   Continuous as evidenced by recording of changes in participation in daily programs
5. The information is:
   Accessible for all disciplines in the client/resident record
   Retrievable from record-keeping systems

The National Association of Activity Professionals has developed three (3) categories of activities which reflect the essential philosophy of basing programming on individual residents needs rather than specific types of activities. These categories are referred to as **Supportive, Maintenance, and Empowerment Activities**.

Supportive activities promote a comfortable environment while providing stimulation or solace to clients/residents who cannot benefit from either maintenance or empowerment activities. These activities are generally provided to residents who may be severely physically or cognitively impaired and/or are unable to tolerate the stimulation of a group program. Examples are: playing soft music, placing colorful objects in a resident's room, and providing tactile or olfactory stimulation (Perschbacher, 1986).

Maintenance activities will vary from one facility to another, but their primary function is to provide resident with a schedule of events that promotes the maintenance of physical, cognitive, social, spiritual, and emotional health. These activities are provided to residents with a variety of functioning levels. Examples include: exercise groups, sports, etc., to improve physical functioning; discussion groups, current events, etc., to improve cognitive functioning; pet therapy, volunteer service, etc., to improve emotional functioning; and participation in life review, religious services, etc., to enhance spiritual functioning.

Empowerment activities emphasize the promotion of self-respect by providing opportunities for self-expression, choice, and social and personal responsibility. These programs differ from maintenance activities in that they assist clients/residents directly in redeveloping a sense of purpose in their lives. Examples include: self-government, cooking, gardening, resident volunteer programs, and creative activities.

In addition, activities are classified into two types: **passive** and **active**.

Passive activities require no participation or response from client/resident; almost all **supportive** activities would be passive.

Active activities require participation and response from the client/resident. This might be an oral response, some physical action or movement, or it might involve some action over a period of time. Most **maintenance** and **empowerment** activities would be active.

STANDARD 2

The analysis of the client/resident needs and strengths are derived from the Activity Assessment.

Rationale:
The data collected for the analysis is used as the baseline for determining the needs that can be filled through activities that enable each resident to attain or maintain the high(est) practicable level of physical, mental, or psychological well-being.

Criteria:
1. The client's/resident's past, present and future activity interests and levels are identified.
2. The client's/resident's present and past health status is identified.
3. The client's/resident's capabilities and limitations are identified.
4. The client's/resident's needs are formulated from the completed Activity Assessment.

STANDARD 3

The Activity Plan is developed based on the client's/resident's strengths and needs.

Rationale:
The client's/resident's strengths and needs are used to develop goals and objectives.
Criteria:
1. Goals are mutually set with the client/resident whenever possible.
2. Goals are set to maximize life satisfaction of the client/resident.
3. Goals are incorporated into the interdisciplinary care plans.
4. Goals and objectives are measurable and realistic.